SACRED AYAHUASCA

A GUIDE TO WISDOM & HEALING

JACQUELINE GRACE

Copyrighted Material

Sacred Ayahuasca: A Guide to Wisdom & Healing
Copyright 2022 by Sacred Vine Press LLC

All Rights Reserved.

No part of this publication may be reproduced, stored in a retrieval system or transmitted, in any form or by any means- electronic, mechanical, photocopying, recording or otherwise- without prior written permission from the publisher, except for the inclusion of brief quotations in a review.

For information about this title or to order other books and/or electronic media, contact the publisher:

Jacqueline Grace
JacquelineGrace10@gmail.com
instagram.com/sacredvine

ISBN: 979-8-218-16516-1

Printed in the United States of America

Author Jacqueline, with Mama Marlene Guatatuca, Warmi Yachak (Medicine Woman), Tribal Eder

For over twenty years, Jacqueline has cultivated a deep spiritual practice rooted in entheogens, as well as meditation, yoga asana, meditation, and pranayama. Combining all of these modalities has allowed for a well-rounded and greater understanding and awareness of nature, people and the Universe. Having experienced ayahuasca all over the world, including the jungles of Ecuador, Costa Rica, Peru, and in local ceremonies in the United States, Jacqueline has provided keen insights on the ins and outs of this beautiful healing medicine.

Contact Jacqueline at JacquelineGrace10@gmail.com or follow @sacredvine on Instagram!

Disclaimer

The information presented in this book details the author's personal experiences with and opinions about the consumption of ayahuasca and other Amazonian plant medicines. The content of this book is for informational purposes only and does not constitute health or medical advice, nor is it intended to diagnose, treat, cure, or prevent any condition or disease. Seek advice from your healthcare provider for your physical and mental health concerns prior to taking ayahuasca and other Amazonian plant medicines.

Neither the author, publisher, or any party involved in the making of this book will be liable for damages arising out of or in connection with the use of this book. No representations or warranties are made of any kind with respect to this book or its contents. In addition, the author does not represent or warrant that the information accessible in this book is accurate, complete or current. This is a comprehensive limitation of liability that applies to all damages of any kind, including (without limitation) compensatory; direct, indirect or consequential damages; loss of data, income or profit; loss of or damage to property and claims of third parties.

The statements made about products and services have not been evaluated by the U.S. Food and Drug Administration.

This book is not intended as a substitute for consultation with a licensed healthcare practitioner, such as your physician. Before you begin any healthcare program, or change your lifestyle in any way, consult your physician or another licensed healthcare practitioner to ensure that you are in good health and that the examples contained in this book will not harm you.

This book provides content related to physical and/or mental health issues. As such, use of this book implies your acceptance of this disclaimer.

Sacred Ayahuasca: A Guide to Wisdom & Healing

Table of Contents

Page 11	Foreword by Dr. Scott Irwin, PhD, CTTS
Page 15	Introduction
Page 25	Chapter 1: What Is Ayahuasca & How It Works
Page 41	Chapter 2: The Sanctity of Life: Medical, Psychological and Safety Considerations
Page 59	Chapter 3: The Way of the Wise Psychonaut: Navigating the Dark Side of Ayahuasca
Page 79	Chapter 4: The Ayahuasca Dieta & Why It Is Important
Page 105	Chapter 5: Other Preparations for an Ayahuasca Ceremony
Page 123	Chapter 6: The Power of Intentions & How to Create Effective Ones

Sacred Ayahuasca:
A Guide to Wisdom & Healing

Table of Contents

Page 135	Chapter 7: What to Expect in Ceremony
Page 155	Chapter 8: What Am I Going to Feel
Page 185	Chapter 9: What Is a Purge & Why It Is Necessary
Page 209	Chapter 10: Plant Medicines that Support Ayahuasca
Page 251	Chapter 11: How Ayahuasca Heals
Page 269	Chapter 12: What to Expect After Ceremony: Integration, Healing & Your New Beginning
Page 287	Chapter 13: This Is the End, Or Is It?
Page 289	Definitions
Page 297	Ayahuasca Journal
Page 303	Citations / References

Foreword
by Dr. Scott Irwin, PhD, CTTS

It is a privilege to introduce Jacqueline Grace's illuminating new book, *Sacred Ayahuasca: A Guide to Wisdom and Healing*. Her guide is an in-depth exploration into the sacred journey of spiritual healing that comes from ayahuasca. With her extensive knowledge and experience with ayahuasca, she guides us through every aspect one must consider before partaking in such a sacred practice - from traditional wisdom to fascinating personal experiences as well as scientific research for those seeking greater insight. Jacqueline has crafted a brilliant guide to provide the tools for a meaningful transformation. Her work is sure to be an invaluable resource for anyone's journey with ayahuasca.

As a passionate integration psychologist and host of healing ayahuasca retreats in the Amazon, I personally feel incredibly blessed to have the opportunity of accompanying thousands of people on their healing journeys through ayahuasca. It has been a privilege watching them unlock new potentials and emerge from this work with a better understanding of themselves, as well as newfound clarity about life's direction for them. Jacqueline is a perfect example; her profound courage and dedication lead to a truly extraordinary transformation. She faced her worries about ayahuasca with openness, allowing herself to be guided by the sacred medicine - even though this may have been daunting at first. Through repeated engagements, she was able to move past her fears and unlock its incredible gifts. Jacqueline has gone above and beyond her own experience with ayahuasca to now offer support, guidance, and understanding for those who wish to explore a similar journey. Jacqueline is innovating traditional wisdom in finding out what makes ayahuasca so life-changing. Her story reminds us that we all possess the power within ourselves for healing and meaningful change.

Jacqueline's story demonstrates the remarkable potential of ayahuasca for personal growth and transformation, but its impact extends far beyond her individual experience. At Sacha Wasi Retreat Centre, we deeply respect the ancient and sacred cultural heritage of indigenous communities such as the Kichwa tribe, who have revered ayahuasca for generations. As a tribute to this invaluable history, we donate 100% of our profits to provide essential resources that support the well-being of these communities in Ecuador. Our efforts range from critical infrastructure projects to ensuring access to basic necessities such as food and clean water. Jacqueline's journey and insight throughout this book is a testament to the power of connection and transformation that ayahuasca can inspire. By supporting the indigenous people and preserving an ancient tradition, we can all benefit from something truly extraordinary.

Ayahuasca can be a powerful healing tool, and in order to maximize its benefits and use it safely, thorough preparation is essential. This book provides the guidance needed for an ultimately informed and transformative experience with ayahuasca: everything from instructions on physical and mental preparations beforehand, to the powerful practice of integration afterward. Experienced in plant medicine herself, Jacqueline has presented reliable insight that makes her guide truly invaluable – helping people make their journey into ayahuasca with accurate information and a deeper understanding of its significance.

I feel immensely proud to be part of the professional development of individuals like Jacqueline, encouraging them to become facilitators and fully certified integration coaches at various plant medicine centers around the world. To ensure they were well equipped upon completion, many of these amazing folks had gone through extensive training programs – providing them with all the essential skills necessary for a successful plant medicine practice. The increased quality assurance process within our global community is essential for continued growth and progress which makes me incredibly excited and passionate about being involved in Jacqueline's guide for ayahuasca.

Jacqueline has opened up a window of opportunity to those around the world by sharing her wisdom and experience with ayahuasca. As an experienced plant medicine practitioner, I'm honored to contribute to this attentive guide that is giving insight to many generations to come who are in search of inner healing. I am thrilled to be part of Jacqueline's work in bringing the knowledge and power of ayahuasca into focus. Every individual has a unique connection to this sacred medicine, allowing them to gain profound experiences and insight through their journey with it. One can certainly rely on *Sacred Ayahuasca: A Guide to Wisdom & Healing* as an informative foundation for anyone looking at going down this transformative jungle medicine path.

Introduction

Who am I to write a book about ayahuasca, and why do I deserve your attention beyond this point? I am not a doctor. I am not a scientist or a researcher in an Ivy League university. I am definitely not a guru. I am not even a shaman (yet). However, I will tell you who I am and why I deserve your attention...

I am you.

I have been curious, yet afraid of consuming this medicine called ayahuasca.

I have asked the same questions you find yourself asking, and I have heard thousands more.

I wanted to experience healing, but after listening to and reading about personal accounts that seemed rather far out and incredibly scary, I wondered if ayahuasca was right for me.

I had friends and relatives give me grief about my decision to consume ayahuasca, and at times, I wondered if perhaps their concerns had merit.

I have walked into an ayahuasca ceremony, wide-eyed, heart pounding, palms sweaty, having absolutely no idea what was about to come my way.

Yet, regardless of the fear and unknowingness, I knew the opportunity to consume this sacred medicine had the potential to change my life for the better. It would appear that we are not only drawn to other humans, but to experiences as well. For some, it is hard to refute the inexplicable pull towards this medicine.

I wrote this book because I believe that with more information, the confusion, stress, and apprehension about consuming ayahuasca can be alleviated. What I offer in these pages are the answers to the many questions you may have, or haven't even thought about, as well as allay your concerns. Having been part of hundreds of ceremonies, I have not only had my own unique experiences, but have collected countless anecdotes of other people's work with ayahuasca, truly marveling at the similarities and the differences. I sat with many shamans, asking questions sand listening intently to every word they shared. Cultivating this information and transforming it into this ayahuasca guide was inspired by the spirit of the medicine Herself, having told me to write this book during several ceremonies. There is no book out there quite like this one. I took great care articulating the knowledge I received from Her and am honored to even breathe Her name.

About Me

I have always been a seeker. Not a thrill seeker, a spiritual seeker! Like most seekers, a desire to know more makes me restless most of the time, constantly questioning life, death, and hereafter. It is a self-perpetuating and endless pursuit, but I know no other way.

Raised Roman Catholic, I was indoctrinated in the belief that Jesus Christ was our Lord and Savior and that I had to surrender to Him for absolution. In my early 20s, I became a born again Christian delving deeper into the religion, whose teachings are very clear; Without being "saved," souls are doomed to eternal damnation. Somewhere deep inside, my spirit and body would not allow me to fully believe these tenets, and the religion eventually became incongruous with my spirit.

In my 30s, I started practicing seated meditation and yoga asana, meeting a wider circle of spiritual people with varied beliefs and ways of living. After some struggle (and a full-on identity crisis),

I completely let go of my Christian indoctrination and started learning more about the nature of the Universe and love. Leaving a religion I was so heavily immersed in and identified with was frightening, but it was the right direction for me.

I am not sure when I first heard the word ayahuasca or when I learned about its effects and possibilities, but my yearning for it started several years before I consumed it. Ayahuasca would drift into my thoughts from time to time, like gentle perfume in the air. When the yearning became more intense, I did significant research, listening, watching, and reading anything on the subject I could get my hands on. In conversation, a friend told me about a resort in Costa Rica where she had a great ayahuasca experience, and so with great excitement, I finally booked a retreat.

I told very few people of my intentions to drink ayahuasca for several reasons. I still find it difficult to wrap my head around this, but there are some forms of pure unadulterated nature that are actually illegal. Like, wind-up-in-jail-for-decades, life-ruined illegal. In addition to ayahuasca, psilocybin mushrooms, peyote, San Pedro, and iboga, for instance, are not only completely misunderstood but can land you in jail in most parts of the world. These substances grow out of the ground, for goodness' sake!

Completely pure. Not processed with chemicals or altered in any way. While plant medicine has come a long way, it is very far from receiving the honor and reverence it deserves.

There also continues to be quite a negative stigma and tremendous misinformation when it comes to consuming psychedelics. I have talked to many people who had to lie to their bosses for fear of losing their jobs, to their partners for fear of ending their relationship, and to their families who would impose such judgment and ridicule it would not be worth the conversation. The truth is, this is a very personal decision that is yours, and yours alone. You have nothing to prove to anyone.

For me, the decision to consume ayahuasca was a no-brainer. While the ego part of me tried to convince the rest of me not to do this unknown crazy thing, I was aware of it and persevered. The doubts the ego imparts, the scenario of disaster it presents, the anxiety that permeates; I am not going to lie, I did struggle to overcome and move past it.

You see, the ego is fickle. Its only job in life is to keep you alive. And quiet. And safe. However, while you are definitely safe(er) sitting in your living room every night, you are not learning. You are not growing. You are not developing. Your truest gift – your light – is not illuminated to its greatest potential. We spiritual seekers are not okay with that!

The nights leading up to my first ayahuasca journey had been devoid of any deep sleep. I certainly prepared ahead of time, learned all I could, and readied myself physically, emotionally, and spiritually--even for the possibility of inadvertently shitting oneself. (Unless you are an infant, is there really any other way to shit oneself?) What was in store for my personal journey, I had no way of knowing.

Many believe that ayahuasca calls to some, and that we are actually chosen to consume and are part of a bigger picture to use it to move humanity's consciousness. While I am not sure about that, I do know consuming this sacred plant medicine is a leap of faith. The **calling** to consume ayahuasca is very personal. One thing is for sure though, if you do decide to consume the medicine, your life and perspective will change. This decision requires you to open your mind, abandon what you have been taught so far about psychedelics, and lean into whatever comes up.

It is also important to elucidate that this is truly an unprecedented time to be alive with such incredible access to the medicine. If you felt the calling to consume ayahuasca in decades past, it would be incredibly challenging and unsafe to access this medicine. Imagine: No Google. No word of mouth. Finding your way in a foreign country with no GPS, through the jungle, perhaps taking a river canoe for hours being attacked by mosquitos, only to find an indigenous tribe and partake in the medicine in the most primitive of conditions.

I believe there is something very special going on in the world right now. People speak of "global ascension" or "global awakening" and there is a definite perceptible shift and increased interest in spiritual pursuits. We know the Universe is always in expansion mode, and humanity has collectively been seeking spiritual knowledge since the dawn of time. However, technology has enabled more people to connect with one another, share their stories, and support each other's awakenings. We are finally starting to understand that we can not only live happy lives, but it is our birthright. This is most definitely an incredible time to be alive!

About Sacred Ayahuasca: A Guide to Wisdom & Healing

Sacred Ayahuasca: A Guide to Wisdom & Healing is a tactical guide to the medicine and to the experience of consuming it. I am not going to talk with you in fancy mystical terms. I will explain what ayahuasca actually is and how it works, who should steer clear of the medicine, how to find a safe place to consume, how to prepare body, mind and spirit for the medicine, what to expect during an ayahuasca ceremony, what other jungle medicines may be used during ceremony, and post ceremony care. Equipped with this information, perhaps I would have felt more at peace walking into my first ceremony.

I may at times personify ayahuasca, and reference a feminine form such as She or Her. Traditionally, the names of gods and goddesses are capitalized and through my direct experience, I believe She deserves this reverence. I certainly hope I do not offend my readers, but I feel this decision deeply in my heart and must honor it.

I also refer to ayahuasca quite frequently as a teacher and as a medicine, as that is how the indigenous peoples know Her. I hold deep cultural appreciation, understanding and respect for the tribes who share their knowledge, their medicine, and their gifts.

It is a practice and a kindness I hope we can all embrace and learn from.

If you are considering ayahuasca in your future, or you have consumed the medicine before and still have questions, read on. If you would like a friend or family member to consider ayahuasca, this book may also help them understand the medicine more fully and make an informed decision.

Please know that ayahuasca is not a recreational drug taken for pleasure, entertainment, relaxation, or escapism. I cannot stress this enough. This medicine requires us to face who we are, the things we have done in our lives, and our trauma. It does not allow us to suppress issues and escape reality. If you want to party, go to happy hour. This is the hardest work you will ever do, and you will thank yourself for it.

There is most definitely a lot to unpack when talking about ayahuasca and there are several ways you can leverage the material in this book. You can certainly read this book from cover to cover, which would be my recommendation. However, if it makes more sense to skip to specific chapters that resonate with you, by all means do so. This book provides a tremendous amount of information that took years to culminate so take your time. She is worth it! And so are you!

Chapter 1
What Is Ayahuasca & How It Works

The term ayahuasca originates from the Quechua words 'aya', meaning soul or spirit, and 'waska', meaning rope or vine. Ayahuasca has hundreds of names, but here are some of the most prevalent:

Grandmother	The Vine of Souls
Mother Ayahuasca	Universe
Pachamama[1]	The Divine
Santo Daime	Life Force
Yagé (also Yajé, Yahé)	Mother Earth
God / Goddess	Caapi
La Medicina / The Medicine	Chacruna
La Purga	Hoasca / Oasca
The Tea	DMT
The Vine	Mado
The Vine of the Dead	Sacrament

Ayahuasca is at times referred to as an entheogen (en·thē·o·gen), which comes from two words of ancient Greek: éntheos and genésthai.[2] Entheos translates to "full of the god, inspired, possessed," and is the root of the English word enthusiasm. Genesthai means "to come into being," or "to become." Entheogen literally means generating the divine within! There are many plant medicines that fall under the entheogen umbrella, such as cannabis, psilocybin mushrooms, peyote, San Pedro, LSD, morning glories, kava, and iboga.

Ayahuasca may also be referred to and act as an adaptogen.[3] Adaptogens in herbal medicine are substances which help the body adapt to stress and exert a normalizing effect upon bodily processes. Adaptogens are typically the root part of the herb. There are many adaptogens; some well-known examples are panax ginseng root, rhodiola rosea root, ashwagandha root, turmeric, moringa, maca, liquorice root, and astragalus root. The DMT found in ayahuasca has been shown to increase the survival rate of neurons and other cell types during acute hypoxia (when bodily tissues do not have enough oxygen) or under chronic oxidative stress (a bodily condition that occurs when antioxidant levels are low).

Ayahuasca (like all psychedelics) is classified as a psychoactive, which in simplest terms is a substance that affects the mind or behavior. There are a lot of everyday substances that fall under this category, including coffee, chocolate, alcohol, nicotine, and cannabis. Ayahuasca is not classified as a psychotropic substance. While psychotropics affect the mind, these are generally prescribed drugs used in tandem with psychotherapy. While ayahuasca is classified as a hallucinogen, having tremendous experience with the medicine, I often wonder why. The word *hallucinogen* indicates delusions and entirely false perceptions. However, those who consume ayahuasca are generally aware they are under the effects of a psychedelic and that it will wear off. Typically, there is no break from reality. While you may see your physical world illuminated, altered or imbued with unseen-before qualities, you are experiencing the reality of the physical world. It is your true environment. Nothing is going to spring up out of nowhere, and there are definitely no pink elephants!

There are three types of psychedelics: Tryptamines, Phenethylamines, and Lysergamides. These three broad categories of psychoactives are naturally occurring chemical compounds.[4] Psychoactives that fall in the tryptamine category include ayahuasca, DMT, psilocybin, Bufo alvarius, and iboga. Psychoactives that fall in the phenethylamine category include amphetamines, methamphetamines and MDMA, along with a long list of synthetic psychedelics such as 2C-B, 2C-E, and 2C-T-7. LSD is both a lysergamide and a tryptamine.

How an Ayahuasca Brew Is Made

Ayahuasca is made from the leaves of the Psychotria viridis shrub along with the Banisteriopsis caapi vine (ayahuasca vine).[5] Psychotria viridis and Banisteriopsis caapi both have hallucinogenic properties but are not really psychoactive unless combined.

The Psychotria viridis leaves (also referred to as chacruna or yagé) contain many alkaloids, but the primary compound is known as N,N-dimethyltryptamine, or DMT for short. This naturally occurring powerful psychedelic substance found in the plant has low bioavailability. Therefore, when ingested, the DMT gets rapidly broken down in the liver and gastrointestinal tract by enzymes called monoamine oxidases (MAO). For this reason, in order for the DMT found in the leaves to be effective, it must be combined with an MAO inhibitor (MAOI). The Banisteriopsis caapi vine contains potent MAOIs called β-carbolines, which also have psychoactive effects of their own. MAO inhibition is crucial as without the β-carbolines, the DMT would be broken down before crossing the blood-brain barrier.[6]

To recap, an ayahuasca brew typically includes:

- Leaves of the Psychotria viridis shrub (chacruna or yagé)
    - Contains N,N-dimethyltryptamine (DMT), which is a powerful psychedelic substance
- Banisteriopsis caapi vine (ayahuasca vine)
    - Powerful MAO inhibitor (MAOIs) called β-carbolines, which allow DMT to take effect

Ayahuasca is sometimes referred to as yagé or Santo Daime. Think of it as a brand name, if you will. The most common understanding of these terminologies is that ayahuasca is from Peru, yagé is from Colombia, and Santo Daime is from Brazil.

While an ayahuasca brew typically contains the Psychotria viridis leaves and the ayahuasca vine, each tribe from varying countries has different traditions, prayers, intentions and processes, as well as different leaf to vine ratios, and different recipes, often adding other plant ingredients. These additional plant ingredients, or admixtures, often have psychotropic qualities as well and can be used on their own. For instance, nicotiana rustica leaves are sometimes added to the brew to increase physical purges. Oco yagé can be added to increase the strength or the duration of a journey (or used in lieu of the

Psychotria viridis leaves). Admixtures are determined by the one making the brew for their emetic, analgesic or purgative qualities. So while the basic ingredients are the same, each "brand" of the medicine may have varied effects due to the brew's strength and pharmacological properties.

Typically an ayahuasca brew is prepared by an experienced healer, ideally a shaman, who will also lead, oversee and guard the ayahuasca ceremony. There are several general terminologies that refer to this healer, such as an Ayahuasquero / Ayahuasquera, Curandero / Curandera, Maestro / Maestra, Shaman, Taita, or Vegetalista. The subject of shamanism will be later expanded upon in this chapter.

To make an ayahuasca brew, the shaman begins by cultivating the ingredients they wish to use. There are several ways to prepare ayahuasca, but customarily the shaman will clean and mash the ayahuasca vines into smaller pieces to increase the extraction of its medicinal compounds. The vine and the leaves are added in layers to a pot of boiling water for ten hours to days. Throughout the entire process, from the gathering of the ingredients to the completion of the brewing, the shaman maintains energetic purity and blesses the medicine with prayers and songs. The end result: a beautiful pot of ayahuasca tea!

Brews vary in taste and thickness and each have their own character and effects. Depending on the balance of ingredients, preparation, and intentions added by the shaman, some brews may bring more visualizations while others will be better for physical purges. I have consumed ayahuasca that was sweet and watery, and others that are thick like molasses and truly took a concerted effort to swallow. (I am not complaining. I always go up for more.)

The Traditional Usage of Ayahuasca in the Amazon

When it comes to this literal mind-blowing concoction, I cannot help but marvel that out of tens of thousands of trees and shrubs found in the rainforest, our earliest indigenous tribes knew to combine these two particular ingredients.[7] As we know, the leaves and the vine that together make this brew are more or less inert individually. Moreover, there are about 80,000 deciduous plant species in the Amazon rainforest, of which more than 10,000 are vines. Somehow these healers choose from that abundance of flora to prepare this psychoactive decoction. The odds of getting this particular combination are absolutely staggering! While it is still a mystery, the elder shamans of the Amazon believe the plants spoke to their ancestors, guiding them to find and appropriately prepare an ayahuasca brew.

Ayahuasca originates predominantly from the Amazonian regions of Colombia, Peru, Ecuador, Costa Rica, Brazil, Bolivia, and Venezuela, and has been used by the indigenous peoples for at least 2,500 years.[8] Nowadays, ayahuasca is grown all over the world in tropical climates. While the leaves of the Psychotria viridis shrub can be ready for harvest in two or three years, the ayahuasca vine takes a minimum of five years to mature. With the growing consumer demand, sustainability is concerning and supply issues are starting to arise. Thankfully, there is increased awareness of this issue and there are several organizations seeking to counter the trend of over-harvesting ayahuasca and the devastating effects of industrial development and agricultural practices that undermine the forest ecosystem in which the plant medicine grows.

There are dozens (or more) of ethnic groups throughout these regions who have utilized ayahuasca in their healing and spiritual traditions.[9] The following is a very incomplete list of some groups carrying the medicine of ayahuasca to the rest of the world today: the Shipibo-Conibo of Peru; the Cofán, Inga, Siona, Coreguaje, and Kamëntsá of Colombia; the Yawinawá and Huni Kuin of Brazil; and the Achuar, Kichwa, and Shuar of Ecuador.

The historical use of ayahuasca among Amazonian indigenous peoples is rooted in the practice of shamanism.[10] Shamanism predates all religions and is found in every pre-modern culture around the world. It is a healing spiritual tradition and way of life based on a deep connection with nature and the many spiritual levels of the cosmos. In traditional cultures, the shaman wears several hats familiar to our modern society: doctor, priest, scientist, and visionary. The shaman is gifted with abilities to connect deeply with the spirits of nature (in plants, animals, water, fire, and so on) and with spirits in other dimensions. The shaman uses techniques such as consuming plant medicines, chanting, singing, humming, whistling, drumming, dancing, fasting, praying, or meditating to journey to the spirit realms to enlist support for healing, gain divinatory information such as where the herds of game are moving or which member of the tribe is causing conflict, and learn the mythological structures and moral values that maintain the tribe's balance amidst nature and the Universe at large.

While there are spiritual and mystical connotations to the term shaman, they are not necessarily tied to a specific religion or creed. In fact, while there may be a number of religions which have evolved from shamanic tradition, and some shamans may identify with an organized religion, shamanism is a spiritual practice.

Many shamans come from a long lineage of shamans, some going back many generations. The knowledge, history, and gifts are passed down, sometimes over thousands of years. Shamans are said to be born into their role and cannot simply become one by willing it to be so. It is not the shaman who summons up the spirits but they, the spirits, who choose her or him. It is a long arduous road to becoming a shaman, one many are incapable of even comprehending.

Through decades of extensive training, a powerful shaman understands that the material world is an expression of a subtler energetic realm, and they can interact with both realms simultaneously. In her book, "An Encyclopedia of Shamanism," author Christina Pratt shares that a shaman by definition is someone who has mastered three specific things: 1) being able to access and return from altered states of consciousness with control, 2) mediating between and understanding the needs of the spirit and physical worlds in a way that can be understood by the community, 3) to be in service of the community in ways other practitioners (such as doctors, priests, and healers) cannot.

It is believed that historically, many shamans would not serve ayahuasca directly to the people. Rather, a person would visit their local shaman, explain their physical or psychological issue, and the shaman would drink for them. The patient would remain present while the shaman addresses the energetic and spiritual aspect of their illness by making journeys into the astral or spirit world to heal them.

A traditional ayahuasca ceremony may have looked like this: The shaman had a conversation with the patient and then performed a diagnostic scan to understand their emotional, energetic, or physical illness. Next, the shaman would drink ayahuasca. Over the course of hours, the shaman would interact with plant or astral spirits to heal the patient. For the Shipibo healer, special songs learned from the plant spirits would be used as a tool to aid in the process of healing.

The spread of ayahuasca to the Western modern world since the late 20th century marks the turning of a new age, one where ordinary people like me and you are invited to be active participants in our healing and shamanic journey. We are beyond privileged to receive from the indigenous Amazonian people their gracious sharing of thousands of years of expert knowledge in the healing arts of ayahuasca. With the help of master-shamans who carry the knowledge of their ancestors, we are invited to encounter ayahuasca personally, learning how to heal ourselves, align with our life purpose, and live in harmony with nature and each other.

Healing Properties

Though ayahuasca was traditionally used for spiritual purposes by indigenous tribes and specific populations, it has become popular worldwide among those who seek a way to treat addiction, recover from PTSD, anxiety, and depression, heal from past traumas, expand the mind, or to simply experience an ayahuasca journey. It is a pleasure to see the early stages of research proving scientifically that this medicine can support improved emotional and physical health and may benefit brain health in a number of ways. Ayahuasca's healing properties will be discussed in greater depth in Chapter 11 but below is a sampling of current research conclusions:[11]

- Both DMT and β-carbolines have been shown to exhibit neuroprotective and neurorestorative qualities in some studies.

- DMT activates the sigma-1 receptor (Sig-1R), a protein that blocks neurodegeneration and regulates the production of antioxidant compounds that help protect brain cells.

- Harmine, the main β-carboline in ayahuasca, has been found to have anti-inflammatory, neuroprotective, and memory-boosting effects in test-tube and animal studies. It has also been observed to increase levels of brain-derived neurotrophic factor (BDNF), a protein that plays an important role in nerve cell growth and promotes nerve cell survival.

- Ayahuasca may improve psychological well-being by increasing the mindfulness capacity of the brain. These effects are mostly attributed to the DMT and β-carbolines present in the brew.

- Ayahuasca also shows very promising results for the treatment of addiction, anxiety, treatment-resistant depression, and post-traumatic stress disorder (PTSD).

The risk of developing a physical dependence or addiction to ayahuasca is incredibly low.[12] This is not unique to ayahuasca, as most psychedelics are generally categorized as non-addictive. To date, no peer-reviewed evidence demonstrates that consuming ayahuasca leads to a tolerance. However, because addiction is not always limited to physical dependency, a behavioral addiction to the experience of using ayahuasca can still occur.

While ayahuasca may at times be a bitter medicine that brings us face-to-face with repressed emotions and inner demons, this plant medicine is virtually impossible to overdose on. There are a handful of animal studies indicating that a lethal dose of DMT in humans would amount to twenty times more than that served in ceremony.[12] There have been reported casualties as a result of ayahuasca consumption, however they are often the result of recipients being dishonest about certain medical conditions or the contraindicated medicines they are taking, or consuming the medicine in inappropriate, unsupervised settings. Get acquainted with who should avoid ayahuasca in Chapter 2 and read up on how to choose a safe retreat space in Chapter 3.

A Western Ayahuasca Ethic

As we in the United States, Europe, and elsewhere benefit from Amazonian indigenous people's sharing of the sacred ayahuasca medicine, we must be aware of the impact we are having on their way of life. With ayahuasca becoming mainstream in all parts of the world, thousands upon thousands of people are flocking to Central and South America and elsewhere to drink the medicine. Some have justly raised critical voices about the effects of Western tourism on previously isolated tribes such as the Shipibo of Peru. With Western presence, such cultures are in danger of becoming integrated into the "development" model of global capitalism. We should not only recognize the priceless gifts that the Amazonian carriers of ayahuasca pass onto us, but also reflect on the impact and ultimate cost they incur by our presence.

As you plan your journey of healing with ayahuasca, perhaps you can consider how to lessen any negative impact and to give back to the tribes. Inquire how your retreat center cares for and supports indigenous people of the area and their policies on how to best protect their land and resources. It is ideal to proceed in right relationship all throughout your healing journey with master plant teachers like ayahuasca. You will always be the student, the humbled one from the West who crawled back to the garden for healing.

The Amazon is the world's most precious depository of plant medicine and is the most concentrated domain of the Gaian mind. By receiving the healing gifts of ayahuasca, you will become obliged to serve the will of Mother Earth in healing the forests and ensuring the preservation of ancient wisdom through indigenous cultures.

An Ayahuasca Recap

What is ayahuasca? It is an entheogen, an adaptogen, a psychoactive, a tryptamine, a mind-blowing concoction that was whispered into the ears of our ancestors by the spirits. She is pure concentrated liquid nature, a consciousness, a spirit, a goddess, a healer, an oracle from beyond. She is an essence without shape. Beyond thought, rationale, emotion, or physical form. Ayahuasca is a master plant medicine. A teacher. The truest love you may ever feel. The swiftest kick in the ass you never knew you needed!

What ayahuasca isn't? It is not a religion, a cult, a magic bullet or a cure all. She is not a feel-good drug or a means of escape. She is not to be disrespected or abused.

You cannot ignore that this medicine is quite complicated. In different Amazonian languages, the word for poison is the same word for medicine. The distinction is not articulated, because in my opinion, the same thing that can cure you can also harm you. The same knife you use to slice oranges is the same knife that can draw blood. It boils down to consuming ayahuasca responsibly, with knowledge, intention and reverence.

In this book, I will help you do that.

Chapter 2
The Sanctity of Life: Medical, Psychological and Safety Considerations

As with any plant medicine, there are several important considerations and best practices to ensure your safety and for the best possible outcome. The unfortunate reality is there are people who absolutely should not consume ayahuasca due to physical, psychological, or pharmacological contraindications. While these people may need healing, consuming ayahuasca may amount to physical or medicinal incompatibility.

It is imperative to adhere to the following protocols for your safety and for the safety of others. If these recommendations are disregarded, ayahuasca is not only dangerous but it could be lethal. I am sorry to sound grim, but there is an expression in the community "You lie, you die!" And that expression needs to be taken seriously. Many people who have had serious and deadly reactions to ayahuasca were simply not truthful beforehand about their medical conditions and the medications they take.

Certain physical contraindications have a higher risk factor for fatalities or negative side effects. Specifically, the most important contraindications to recognize are hypertension (high blood pressure), cardiac disease, and liver failure. Ayahuasca can elevate blood pressure. As such, those who already suffer from high blood pressure and cardiac conditions are at higher risk for heart attacks and strokes among other possible complications. Additionally, ayahuasca is processed through the liver and the added stress on that organ could be potentially dangerous in people with advanced stages of liver disease. You should not consume ayahuasca if you have these medical conditions.

The following partial list of physical conditions are contraindicated with ayahuasca:[1]

- Cardiovascular problems including, but not limited to hypertension
- Liver disease
- Pregnant or lactating
- Glaucoma
- Retinal detachment
- Broken bones or fractures
- Recent surgeries
- Acute infectious diseases

- Tuberculosis
- Epilepsy or a history of convulsions
- Cerebrovascular accident
- Gallbladder, kidney or pancreas diseases
- Certain cases of gastroduodenal ulcer or gastritis
- Digestive hemorrhage
- Fever above 99
- Those who have difficulty vomiting

In addition to the above partial list of physical contraindications, those with serious psychiatric conditions should avoid ayahuasca. If you are suffering with mental health, make it a priority to talk with your team of medical professionals and the retreat center to determine if ayahuasca is right for you, as well as the best course of action before, during, and following ceremony. Ayahuasca should not be used as a substitute for psychotherapy or medical care.

The following partial list of psychiatric conditions are contraindicated with ayahuasca:

- Bipolar and related disorders
- Schizophrenia and other psychotic related disorders

(continued...)

- Borderline personality disorder
- Eating disorders
- Severe depression
- Suicidal ideation, intent, and plan
- Nonsuicidal self-injury (self-harm)

There are pharmacological and drug contraindications to understand as well. The use of ayahuasca is contraindicated with a long list of prescription drugs, herbs and substances, especially those which affect the serotonin system. If you are currently taking medication or herbs, or consuming drugs of any kind, you will be required to cease taking them for at least four to six weeks prior to the consumption of ayahuasca. It is imperative that you talk to your team of medical professionals to determine if you qualify to stop taking your medications as well as the best course of action. You must also confer with the retreat center to determine their policies on your specific prescription drugs, herbs and substances.

Here is just a partial overview of pharmaceutical prescription medications, over the counter medications, plant medicines, street drugs, and herbs that are dangerously contraindicated with ayahuasca:[2,3]

- Antidepressants, including Selective Serotonin Reuptake Inhibitors (SSRIs), Serotonin and Norepinephrine Reuptake Inhibitors (SNRIs), and tricyclic antidepressants
- Antianxiety medications, mood stabilizers, antimanic agents, anticonvulsants, and antipsychotics
- Amphetamines, methamphetamines, dextroamphetamines, methylphenidates
- Narcotics (opioids), opiates and psychostimulants, such as oxycodone, hydrocodone, fentanyl, crack, cocaine, and heroin as well as depressant drugs including benzodiazepines, and barbiturates
- Dissociatives, including Ketamine, PCP (angel dust), DXM (lean, dank), nitrous oxide, and methoxetamine
- Psychedelics and mind-altering substances, including psilocybin mushrooms, mescaline, peyote, San Pedro, iboga, LSD, MDMA, bufotenin / Bufo alvarius (5-MeO-DMT)
- Sedatives, both prescription and non-prescription

(continued...)

- Cough and cold medications, decongestants, and allergy medications
- Diet supplements and appetite suppressants
- Herbal preparations and supplements, including boswellia (Indian frankincense), ephedra, ginkgo biloba, ginseng, kanna, kava, kratom, licorice root, nutmeg, rhodiola rosea, scotch broom, sinicuichi, St. John's Wort, and yohimbe

This list is not inclusive of all pharmaceutical medications, drugs and herbs that are contraindicated with ayahuasca. Please talk to your team of medical professionals and the retreat center to get their feedback and specific direction.

While not being able to consume the medicine may be disappointing, consider the history of ayahuasca that was outlined in Chapter 1. It is only in recent times that an abounding number of Westerners became aware of ayahuasca and started coming to the Amazon in droves to experience the medicine themselves, thus changing the model for ayahuasca consumption quite dramatically.

It may be a comfort to know there are still places where shamans will welcome you to attend ayahuasca ceremonies in this older traditional fashion. While you will not consume a full dose of the medicine, some shamans may serve you a tincture that will introduce your body to ayahuasca and allow for healing, albeit at a slower rate. Consider it a microdose of the medicine, if you will. You will be immersed in the energy of the ceremony, which is not only an incredible experience, but also offers a deeper opportunity for healing. Additionally, the shaman can perform a limpia on you, which some may argue when done by a powerful experienced shaman, is more healing than the actual medicine. (A limpia is explained further in Chapter 7.)

I cannot stress this enough. It is your absolute responsibility to inform your team of medical professionals, as well as the facility where you plan to consume ayahuasca of your physical and mental health as well as the medications, drugs, and herbs you may take. If you are not eligible to consume ayahuasca, there are other modalities you can explore that are effective, safer and more appropriate for you. Remember, you lie, you die. It is really that simple.

Menstruation / Moon Cycle

The word menstruation derives from the Latin and Greek word for moon, hence why this is referred to as a moon cycle in the plant medicine community. While a moon cycle technically is the entire month, from day one to day twenty-eight of a woman's full menstrual cycle, most people talk about being on their moon cycle when they are menstruating. Consuming ayahuasca during this sacred time of the month is controversial so I would like to take time to share the origins of the issues and possible contraindications a woman may experience while under the effects of the medicine during menstruation.

Perhaps you will be surprised to learn that most tribes forbid women who are menstruating to participate in an ayahuasca ceremony. I've heard every reason imaginable too. One shaman said women who are menstruating while under the effects of the medicine are more powerful than the shamans and can overpower a ceremony. Another said women who are menstruating while under the effects of the medicine are completely out of control and can endanger others in the ceremony. Seems a little Godzilla-like to me. However, ayahuasca places quite a bit of importance on integrity, so it is important that you honor the space and inform the retreat center and shaman before you consume if you are menstruating.

A little side note, hermana a hermana. You may decide it is really not an ideal time to participate in an ayahuasca ceremony while you are menstruating. An ayahuasca ceremony can be intense, and during this time, you may not be feeling your best. We women know, when the flood gates open there is often physical discomfort, emotional fluctuations, and all kinds of energetic shifts. This time of death and rebirth should be embraced with patience and loving kindness. Postponing your ceremony if you are menstruating is an important consideration because adding ayahuasca to the mix may just make that time one uncomfortable helluva crazy ride.

If your shaman allows for participation in ceremony while you are menstruating, the following recommendations may help:

- The shaman or facility may provide you with a little bit of loose tobacco to place in your naval. Tobacco is a masculine protective powerhouse, and can absorb and deflect negative energies that may circle near your womb.

- Do not wear a tampon. While tampons in general are considered unhealthy, during ceremony it is imperative that nothing is plugged up. Organic pads are a great option.

- Sage can provide protection as well. The leaves of this masculine herb can be sprinkled around your space in the ceremony or you can put some under your pad so He can create a wall of protection between you and the room.

Proper "Set & Setting"

The concept of set and setting was first introduced by Timothy Leary and his colleagues at Harvard and is discussed in their 1964 psychedelic guidebook, *The Psychedelic Experience: A Manual Based on the Tibetan Book of the Dead*. In the simplest terms "set" is your internal mindset and "setting' is your external or physical environment. Paying attention to both set and setting will have a big influence on your ayahuasca experience.

An Elaboration on Set

The term set is a shortened version of "mindset," and it is as complex as the mind itself. Consider it a reflection of your inner climate—your mood, personality, beliefs, perceptions, and so on. While we generally look at set in terms of these categories, it goes much deeper than that. Set refers to your inner climate which can be influenced, shaped, and affected by so many variables.

Mood

The psychiatrist Stan Grof, who has guided or supervised around 4,500 LSD sessions, has described psychedelics as "non-specific amplifiers" of experience.[4] This means they can amplify whatever an individual brings to the table, including their current mood. If you come to the ceremony space in a positive mood and you are excited for what's to come, ayahuasca may enhance this state of mind. However, if you show up anxious, negative, or frustrated, there is a greater chance of having an unpleasant experience.

Keep in mind, ayahuasca is always in charge. You may show up happy as a clam, and She will still kick your ass. However, from a practical matter, if you can focus on the opportunity to explore and be grateful, ayahuasca may amplify that and show you euphoria!

Personality

You can find the HEXACO-PI-R Personality Inventory at hexaco.org, which will help identify your personality. There are six broad categories including: **H**onesty-Humility; **E**motionality; e**X**traversion; **A**greeableness; **C**onscientiousness; **O**penness to Experience. Within each category, there are subsets, with a narrower "facet" scales of the HEXACO-PI-R. Some research may indicate what kind of ayahuasca journey you may have, based on these results.

A study published in the *Journal of Psychoactive Drugs* found correlations between personality traits and certain ayahuasca experiences.[5] For instance, people who fall into the Openness category had a higher rate of experiences including "love, inner visions, and contact with non-ordinary beings and transcendent forces". Meanwhile, extroverted people seemed to experience a deeper sense of connection to other people. Those who are agreeable and have high emotional stability were the least likely to experience fear during a trip. On the flip side, individuals who scored high on the risk-taking measure were more likely to experience ego death or dissolution.

Beliefs

Our mind set also includes our beliefs, whether it be religious, philosophical, cultural, or attitudinal. Religious icons perceived in these altered states vary depending on the person's particular religion. Christians are more likely to interact with Jesus, while Buddhists meet with the Buddha, and so on. Even the imagery people experience during a journey is indirectly reflective of their religious beliefs.

Our pre-existing beliefs on the nature of reality, consciousness, and what ayahuasca is can guide your experience onto different paths. Some people believe ayahuasca contains plant spirits, and, while on the medicine, they can connect to a non-material or spiritual realm. Another person may believe the medicine is an effective tool for introspection and improving mental health. Each person will have their own unique experience based on these pre-existing beliefs.

"Physical Body" Set

While set generally deals with the mind, your physical state plays an important part of your mindset. If you come to ceremony ill, injured, or generally unhealthy, these sensations may get amplified during your journey. Consider waiting for a more suitable time to consume ayahuasca to mitigate your chances of having a negative experience. Also get reacquainted with who should avoid ayahuasca altogether in Chapter 2.

An Elaboration on Setting

When it comes to the physical aspect of setting, there is more than meets the eye. This characteristic refers to all that is going on in the outside world, such as the people around you and their behaviors, the music playing, the smells in the air, the weather, even the cultural forces that are not as readily visible.

Location is a very important facet of setting. Are you in a ceremonial space that is quiet, sacred, and contemplative? Or, are you at Burning Man? Are you in the jungle? Or, are you in a yoga studio in Brooklyn? It is quite possible that if your environment is not purposeful, you may find yourself over-stimulated, overwhelmed and confused. It is imperative that your physical setting supports the contemplative nature of ayahuasca. Ayahuasca *is* nature and She loves a natural setting, free of electricity, electromagnetic fields, and distraction. Being in this environment and connecting with nature while on your ayahuasca journey will enable a feeling that you are a part of Her and the natural world rather than separate from it. If the retreat space supports it and you have the ability and opportunity, get up and walk outside barefoot. Put your hands on the ground. Breathe the fresh air. Listen to and take in the nature that surrounds you. Look up! The stars in the night sky are normally amazing, but when you are on an ayahuasca journey, it is truly an unbelievable sight.

The people in your group can also affect your setting. More times than not, we start a retreat with a group of strangers, and, after the first night of ayahuasca, we are all in love. However, if you find yourself overwhelmed in large crowds or are fearful with strangers, look for retreats that have smaller groups of participants. Some resorts offer semi-private or even private retreats, if you are really looking to minimize the social aspect of your retreat.

Music plays a big role in the setting of an ayahuasca experience. During the midst of your journey, the shaman may share traditional indigenous Amazonian songs called icaros. I cannot think of anything more soothing and supportive than a beautiful icaros and you may find yourself yearning for more! These sacred songs have made me weep with pure love, and I know you will feel the same. The electronic music producer Jon Hopkins timed his latest album, *Music for Psychedelic Therapy*, to last the duration of a ketamine trip. Hopkins states:[6]

Music For Psychedelic Therapy is not ambient, classical or drone but has elements of all three. For me it's a place as much as it is a sound. It works for the sober mind, but takes on a new dimension entirely when brought into a psychedelic ceremony. In my own psychedelic explorations testing this music, I found a quote I had read would keep coming to mind. 'Music is liquid architecture, architecture is frozen music.' I love this idea of music as something you inhabit, something that works on you energetically. In fact, it was while in that state that the title appeared to me. Psychedelic-assisted therapies are moving into legality across the world, and yet it feels like no one is talking about the music; the music is as important as the medicine.

To Conclude: Who Should Not Consume Ayahuasca & Other Considerations

The considerations and best practices I have outlined are good starting points to consider prior to consuming ayahuasca. While there is no definitive rule for who gets the green light, there is a consensus among doctors, shamans, and practitioners that some people should certainly steer clear of ayahuasca until they are experiencing better health circumstances.

If you have found yourself to not have any of the physical or psychiatric conditions or pharmacological and drug contraindications, you may be in a fortunate position to consume this sacred medicine. If you qualify to consume ayahuasca and trust the calling to do so, make sure you are feeling stable and are in a somewhat good place. While this is subjective, know that you will need to be steady as you navigate your spirit side. For some, it can get pretty uncomfortable. Ayahuasca can be a challenging medicine and you want to have the best set and setting, as well as be in optimal physical, mental, and spiritual condition.

Chapter 3
The Way of the Wise Psychonaut: Navigating the Dark Side of Ayahuasca

I love ayahuasca more than most and I will sing its praises to anyone who will listen. While ayahuasca offers life-changing opportunities, there is a dark side to this medicine. With the increase in demand, many new medicine carriers have emerged, including some who should not be trusted with this powerful medicine.

While what I am about to share may change your course of action, consuming ayahuasca is a big deal and you deserve to be well-versed in every regard. This chapter will explore how to find a safe place to consume the medicine and offer questions you can use when qualifying retreat spaces. I will also share some understanding about the dangers of unqualified medicine carriers and how to protect yourself from being exploited. With some understanding, research and planning, you can proceed safely as a wise psychonaut and mitigate the dangers of consuming ayahuasca.

Finding a Safe Place to Consume Ayahuasca

If, after you have determined you are physically and physiologically able to consume ayahuasca, finding an experienced shaman and a safe place to sit with the medicine will be your number one priority.

The business of ayahuasca is certainly booming and there are a fair share of charlatans and untrained facilitators in the guise of spiritual guides. This can be dangerous for those consuming the medicine who may be opening themselves up to the possibility of physical, emotional, and spiritual harm. It is imperative the shaman and support staff are ethically sound, educated, and experienced in the ways of the plant.

Nowadays, you can drink ayahuasca pretty much anywhere in the world. While in the United States, ayahuasca is a Schedule I substance making it illegal under federal law, there are several churches in the country that have religious exemption and have so far operated with impunity such as Santo Daime, União do Vegetal and Barquinha. There are also opportunities to drink ayahuasca in underground ceremonies, often with visiting shamans. Leanna Standish, a professor at the University of Washington School of Medicine, estimated there are one-hundred ayahuasca circles happening every night in just Manhattan alone.[1] I have had some truly wonderful experiences in the United States with visiting shamans that I know and trust.

If you are looking to experience the medicine in Her land, Colombia, Peru, Ecuador, and Costa Rica would be my first choices. Resort accommodations range dramatically from sleeping in tents in the jungle to five-star accommodations. Some have solo sleeping accommodations, while others require sharing a room with one or more participants. Some places serve farm-to-table fresh organic meals, others not so much.

I developed the following questions you may consider asking the retreat center prior to booking your stay. These are simply suggestions, and you do not necessarily need to ask all of them. If I were to prioritize, I highly encourage asking the first series of questions to ensure the person leading your ceremony has extensive experience serving ayahuasca. I have consumed medicine with retreat centers that did not have shamans and I do not recommend it. Regardless of where you choose to drink ayahuasca, make sure you are working with professionals. Again, this medicine should not be taken lightly.

Retreat Questions

Questions Regarding the Shaman

1. Who will be serving the medicine?
    a. What is their history with the medicine?
    b. What is their lineage?
    c. How long have they been serving the medicine in general?
    d. How long have they been serving the medicine at your resort?
    e. How were they trained?
    f. Are they affiliated with a specific tribe?

Questions Regarding the Medicine

2. Who makes the ayahuasca served in ceremony?
    a. (if not the shaman) What connection does the shaman have to those who make the brew?

3. What part of the world does the medicine served in ceremony come from?

4. What type of ayahuasca is served in ceremony (eg: Santo Daime, yagé)?

5. Are there other ingredients added to the brew, in addition to Psychotria viridis leaves and Banisteriopsis caapi (ayahuasca) vine?

6. How is dosing determined?

Questions Regarding the Support

7. Is a doctor available before, during and after ceremony?

8. Is a registered nurse or paramedic available before, during and after ceremony?

9. Has your facility had any participants experience serious medical issues or death during ceremony?

10. How many facilitators generally support each ceremony?

11. Do the shaman and facilitators drink the brew during ceremony?

Questions Regarding the Dieta
(See Chapter 4 for more information on the dieta.)

12. What is your recommended dieta?

13. What medicines, supplements and other items are contraindicated before ceremony?

14. What health conditions are prohibited prior to consuming ayahuasca?

15. Do you have a health intake procedure prior to consuming the medicine? If so, what is involved? Who is it conducted by?

Questions Regarding the Ceremony

16. Will there be an opportunity to talk with the shaman before ceremony?

17. During a particular ceremony, how many times is ayahuasca offered?

18. Can participants request more ayahuasca, beyond what is offered, if needed?

19. Will there be music, live or otherwise, during ceremony?

20. What time does ceremony typically begin and end?

21. What time do participants typically leave the ceremony space following ceremony?

22. Can participants sleep in the ceremony space following ceremony?

23. Will there be fruit or snacks served following ceremony?

24. What is the ceremony space like? Is it partially opened, air conditioned, up/down stairs?

25. What is made available to participants in the ceremony space (for example: bedding, sheets, a bucket, tissues, water, etc.)?

26. Are there any essential items I need to bring to ceremony?

27. Are participant's cell phones taken prior to ceremony? If so, where are they stored and when do they get returned?

28. How many bathrooms are available to the participants during ceremony? How far are they from where we consume the medicine?

29. How much physical space does each participant have in ceremony?

30. What is the protocol for when someone is really struggling in ceremony? Do you remove them from the ceremony space?

31. Are participants permitted to use mapacho (sacred tobacco) during ceremony?

32. Are participants allowed to smoke cigarettes and/or vape? If so, are there designated areas?

Questions Regarding the Retreat Offering & Space

33. What is the cost for the retreat?

34. Is there an additional fee for the medicine, outside of the retreat fee?
    a. If so, how is that paid?

35. What are the sleeping accommodations?

36. Do I have a private bathroom?

37. How many ceremonies are included in the retreat?
    a. (if more than one) Is there more than one kind of brew served throughout the week?

38. What other plants or plant medicines are made available to participants during ceremony?

39. What is the daily schedule?

40. What is the protocol if I choose to leave the retreat early?

41. What kinds of foods are served? Are they in line with the dieta?

42. What kinds of support services do you provide participants before, during, and after ceremony?

43. What is your maximum capacity for participants?

44. What is the average number of participants?

45. How do you honor my privacy?
    a. Is my personal data shared with third-parties?
    b. Are there instances where photos may be taken of me by the resort without my permission and posted online?

Questions Regarding Woman & Menstruation

46. Are menstruating women permitted to participate in ayahuasca ceremonies?
    a. (If no) What are your policies and penalties regarding rescheduling my retreat in the event I am scheduled to get my period during ceremony?

Dangers of Unqualified Medicine Carriers, Brujos, and Exploitation

Ayahuasca is a profoundly powerful medicine for healing, learning, and the evolution of the self and soul, but like all forms of power, in the wrong hands it can be disastrous. There are three main cautionary considerations here: Receiving ayahuasca from an unqualified facilitator; receiving the medicine from a trained but maligned facilitator known as a brujo or sorcerer; and being sexually or psychologically exploited by unscrupulous shamans, facilitators, staff or charlatans.

Unqualified Carriers

The issue of unqualified medicine carriers recently initiated into the ways of ayahuasca is pervasive among Western societies. Western culture loves the "get results quick" path of gratification and transformation, but this is impossible on the path of ayahuasca. True, just one ceremony weekend can change your life forever, but we are wise to listen to indigenous Amazonian elder medicine carriers about the requisite path for becoming a qualified server of ayahuasca. In many Amazonian cultures, the path to become a shaman involves a decade or longer of rigorous training overseen by elder shamans carrying thousands of years of knowledge passed on from their ancestors and is typically not a personal choice, but rather is a calling from the plant Herself.

Today, some Westerners fool themselves into believing that after a few months in retreat they are now qualified to serve the medicine back home. This is incredibly short-sighted and very dangerous. Even with the best intentions, if they lack the expertise of an experienced shaman, they put their ceremony participants at risk of being assaulted by spiritual entities. Ayahuasca, like other psychedelic master plant medicines, brings you into the "metaverse" of the soul, a place like the internet but instead of cyberspace, it is an inner-spiritual space. If you do not have proper safeguards, you may find yourself in worse shape than when you started. Be diligent about the medicine carrier who is serving and facilitating your journey and make sure you do not find yourself in an amateur circle.

Juan Guillermo Chindoy (@taita.juanito on Instagram)

In our tradition, being initiated to the use of a sacred tool is a path of patience, dedication and deep internal work. It is a process that depends on the capacity of the apprentice, their discipline, their dietas and wisdom. This sacred tool will be gifted by their teacher and will enhance their path of healing in a new light.

The Wayra, also known as the Spirit of the Wind may take from 8 - 10 years to be initiated. This sacred tool will be as powerful as the apprentice themselves, as it works as an extension of their being. Meaning, the cleaner the apprentice's light-body and ability to channel nature spirits the more powerful their tool will be.

The Wayra is like a sword and a shield and an antenna. It is an essential tool used during the "limpia" or cleansing process, alongside the chants it assists in the channeling of the healing through the Curandero.

Brujos

Another major concern when consuming the medicine is brujos, who pose as shamans or medicine men/women but are actually either actively intending to exploit you or who are working with spirits that are not intended for healing. Brujos focus on power and are not interested in helping others. They are known for witchcraft, spells, and using powers from the dark side. It may surprise you to learn that a Goddess healer like ayahuasca can be appropriated for anything other than healing and spiritual growth, but this is definitely the case. It seems She grants us free will to choose our intended path.

Indeed, it is naive to think that the history of ayahuasca usage through the past thousands of years has been all benevolent and only for healing. In fact, ayahuasca has long played a vital role in the very complex social dynamics of Amazonian traditional peoples. For instance, Ayahuasquero brujos frequently quarrel and compete with each other for power and status in their societies. It is not uncommon for such brujos to use ayahuasca for psychic warfare, casting curses, and sending psychic darts at each other.

It has also been rumored that brujos can create energetic connections with recipients of their medicine and can take the gifts and wisdom they receive during ceremony. The master healers of the Amazon also sometimes scoff at their brujo neighbors, saying that they gained their power from forming pacts with demonic entities. You know how that story ends! It is never good for the sorcerer.

There is a big difference between one who is a healer and one who has learned techniques of power. The same is true in our society: Knowledge of science can be used to design bombs or to heal diseases.

Exploitation

Brujos are often exploitative, but this covers just one aspect of this issue. More commonly in the West, a major danger affecting retreat guests is sexual exploitation and/or psychological manipulation. Being under the influence of the medicine encompasses difficult moments of collective intense healing and rapid transformation. As a byproduct, many people in these healing and spiritual communities have unresolved histories of trauma and thus sometimes inflict harm upon others. Unfortunately, one of the most common instances of this shadow-expression is in sexual exploitation of retreat guests, more often women.

Especially for those beginning their ayahuasca journey, the medicine experience can make recipients very open, vulnerable and suggestable. There are many cases of unqualified medicine carriers and facilitators who have sexually exploited retreat participants. This is even a problem among some of the indigenous Amazonian medicine carriers. Perhaps they lose touch with their honorable intent after experiencing higher status, power, and wealth in serving the medicine. When an Ayahuasquero breaches the most sacred boundaries of another person, he may find himself penalized by ostracization and the abandonment of his healing spirit helpers. Sexual exploitation is another reason you need to be tremendously careful when choosing who to drink ayahuasca with.

Similarly, psychic manipulation is another red flag to watch out for. After a few ayahuasca journeys where they meet God and embody their Higher Self for a moment, cult-like leaders believe they are Jesus Christ resurrected with the Good News. Charismatic cult leaders with delusions of grandeur can convince vulnerable people in the midst of their healing processes that they know what is best for them. Look for shamans who embody the humility of knowing that they cannot heal you, but only create an optimal environment to facilitate your healing. No one else can heal you. Only *you* can heal yourself!

Last, I offer you a prayer to request guidance from the medicine in leading you to the safest and most perfect ayahuasca ceremony for your highest healing and wellbeing. Use this prayer or create one, but do pray on it from your heart.

Dear Mother Ayahuasca, Please guide me to the perfect ceremony space to consume this powerful sacrament, for my optimal healing and well-being. I wish to receive your highest blessings in complete safety and protection. Thank you.

Be a Wise Psychonaut

Nowadays ayahuasca is being served everywhere, offering each of us the opportunity for deep healing. This is a very new world for the Western mind which has been conditioned over millennia in contexts of trauma and materialism. It seems that in an instant, an entire new Universe has been discovered in our backyard! It is our birthright as human beings on planet Earth to voyage with ayahuasca and work with Her on our spiritual and healing journey, but this process should be approached with caution and respect. Our lives and mental health are on the line when we journey deep into our inter-dimensional space.

It cannot be overstated that you need to be prepared and diligent about who you are trusting with your body, mind, and spirit. Research the retreat center thoroughly. Read reviews. Call the retreat center you are considering, ask many questions, and ensure the medicine carriers are qualified to serve ayahuasca. Talk with friends and family who have had ayahuasca experiences and get their input. And if possible, go with a friend who will have your back.

What you should not do is go to Peru or elsewhere without a plan. Sometimes the "trust the flow" journey works out, but unless you are experienced on this path, it can very easily end in disaster when blindly wandering into the Amazon. There is no downside to carefully mapping your way through this winding path. Doing your due diligence in that regard can lead you safely through a beautiful experience.

You are ultimately the highest source of wisdom for yourself. You discern whether a situation feels sketchy or safe. If you are just beginning your path of ayahuasca, I advise you to combine the intuition of your gut with the rational discernment of your mind.

There are many wonderful medicine carriers now serving ayahuasca all over the world. If you are considering a journey to Central or South America, or anywhere else to receive the medicine from native peoples, be cautious and follow the protocols outlined above. It is always ideal to experience ayahuasca with a trusted retreat center where master healers from indigenous tribes are working in the safest and most supportive environments.

Last, I also cannot overstate the importance of prayer: Pray, pray, pray for protection and guidance. If you humble yourself to the medicine and the Universe, stating your sincere desire for healing and growth, you will be helped along the path. The more sincere and passionately heartfelt your prayer, the more you will receive.

Go forth in safety and love, my friend!

Seeking Professional Support

If you experience a mental health crisis after an ayahuasca experience, seek professional treatment from a trained individual who understands psychedelic and transpersonal experiences.

Check the following resources:

- MAPS Integration List: https://maps.org/take-action/resources/crisis-resources/
- Psychedelic Support: https://psychedelic.support/ for a list of providers in your area.

Chapter 4
The Ayahuasca Dieta & Why It Is Important

Ah, the ayahuasca dieta! I will share what it is, why we do it, and why it matters.

A shamanic dieta is prescribed by a master shaman, often for a purpose such as cultivating a deeper connection with a specific plant medicine, purifying and healing the body, mind and spirit, communicating with ancestors, and developing a relationship with the plant world overall. A shamanic dieta not only heals physical illness, but it also enables learning on how to work with ayahuasca, sensitizes oneself to the plant spirits, builds protections, develops plant allies, gets rid of negative spirits, and heals spiritual diseases.

A traditional shamanic dieta is extremely strict and requires tremendous devotion. Those adhering to a shamanic dieta are not permitted to consume salt, oils, spices, sugar, vegetables, and fruits. A shamanic dieta typically consists only of rice, potatoes, and occasionally a little boiled chicken, fish, plantains or eggs. Definitely no Starbucks and definitely no fun! A shamanic dieta also prohibits sexual release, as well as the use of toothpaste, soaps, deodorant, and shampoos, and is often done in isolation over the course of many months to years.

I hope I didn't lose you. A strict shamanic dieta is not required in the weeks prior to your ayahuasca ceremony. However, you are expected to prepare your body, mind and spirit by not consuming specific foods and doing particular activities, as well as putting your focus on healthy "dieta-minded" consumption. I will continue to refer to this practice as the dieta to honor its origins. The end goal: Be conscious of what you are consuming and doing to serve your highest health and well-being in preparation for the most positive and life-changing experience possible.

We all have energetic bodies and what we consume and how we live greatly affects its frequency. The following diet and lifestyle recommendations and their timelines will:

- Enable a connection with ayahuasca before ceremony, showing Her that you are dedicated to this journey
- Ensure a safer more comfortable experience
- Lessen the types and frequencies of purges
- Minimize toxicity, inflammation and stress

- Purify your body so that you are more receptive to the medicine during ceremony
- Begin a dialogue with Her way before ceremony begins by clearing the mind
- Allow for an enhanced and deeper relationship with ayahuasca
- Create more opportunities for your journey

While there has never been a recorded fatality due to a food interaction with ayahuasca, certain foods are known to increase unpleasant symptoms such as a severe headache (which can last for days), an accelerated heartbeat, or digestive upset. However, I have had conversations with people who only moderately follow the dieta and have wonderful journeys. Determine your own level of dedication to the dieta, as only you know what is best for you. While some recommendations are absolutely required, most of this preparatory work is designed to enhance the experience, not to make yourself crazy.

WARNING: SSRIs & Serotonin Syndrome

Of all the dietary pre-ceremony considerations, the most important is to ensure that you are not taking any contraindicated medications that have effects on the serotonin system, such as

Selective Serotonin Reuptake Inhibitors (SSRIs). If you choose to participate in an ayahuasca ceremony, work with your medical team to help you completely cease use of SSRIs (and other serotonin-affecting medications) six weeks before taking ayahuasca.[1] Failure to do so can cause death from an overwhelming amount of serotonin flooding your system during ayahuasca ceremony, a condition known as "serotonin syndrome."[2]

Contraindicated medications are featured in Chapter 2. Please read that chapter carefully and ensure you are not violating any of those requirements.

What to Avoid

A priority component of the dieta is to avoid foods high in tyramine. Let's break it down in the simplest terms:[3]
- Tyramine is an amino acid that helps to regulate blood pressure.
- Monoamine oxidase (MAO) is an enzyme that breaks down excess tyramine in the body.
- Ayahuasca is a monoamine oxidase inhibitor (MAOI), reducing monoamine oxidase's ability to break down excess tyramine in the body.

Because ayahuasca is an MAOI and reduces the body's ability to break down excess tyramine, there is a potential for increased and possibly dangerous levels of tyramine in the blood, which can cause a severe rise in blood pressure (hypertensive crisis).[4] Symptoms may include severe headache, nausea and vomiting, sweating and severe anxiety, nosebleeds, fast heartbeat, chest pain, changes in vision, shortness of breath, and confusion.

There is a long list of foods, medications, and activities that are recommended to be avoided prior to ceremony. Some should be avoided 30+ days prior to ceremony, others 5+ days prior to ceremony. I will describe each category in detail, and then provide a summary that you can quickly reference when needed.

While the following outline is generally agreed upon, work with your retreat center to follow the dieta they recommend. Every tribe has different recommendations and time frames to follow, according to their tradition and their medicine.

Pre-Ceremony Foods and Activities to Avoid[5,6,7]

All Master Plant Medicines, Hallucinogens (including microdosing), and Street Drugs: Abstain 30+ days prior to ceremony

All entheogens must be avoided at least 30 days prior to ceremony, including but not limited to: psilocybin mushrooms, mescaline, peyote, San Pedro, and iboga. In addition, ketamine, LSD, and MDMA also need to be avoided at least 30 days prior to ceremony. Street drugs such as crack, cocaine, heroin, opioids, methamphetamines (crystal meth), PCP (angel dust) should be avoided for 30+ days prior to ceremony, but hopefully for an eternity.

I am going to talk about cannabis separately because it is such an easy plant to get and is one of the highest medicines consumed recreationally. According to the World Health Organization, about 147 million people (2.5% of the world population) consume cannabis compared with 0.2% consuming cocaine and 0.2% consuming opiates.[8] In the present decade, cannabis abuse has grown more rapidly than cocaine and opiate abuse. Unfortunately, many have forgotten that cannabis is a master plant teacher and do not treat Her with the reverence She deserves. (Yes, cannabis is a divine feminine!) When we abuse cannabis or use it for non-ceremonial contexts, there can be significant harmful effects. Ideally, consume cannabis ceremonially and with intention as a way to better your life and not escape it. Treat Her with as much respect as you give ayahuasca. But do not do so within 30 days of your ayahuasca ceremony.

As a general rule of thumb, every master plant medicine teacher deserves our focus and sufficient space to work. This is not only a practice of respect in honoring the unique spirit of each plant, it is also an optimal way to receive the most healing and learning from the gifts of each medicine.

Pork: Abstain 21+ days prior to ceremony

Pork is highest on the list of foods to avoid prior to consuming ayahuasca. Pigs are incredibly intelligent (and very loving), and understand much more than we believe. They sense when they are about to be slaughtered which produces a tremendous amount of stress and adrenaline in their bodies. This stress and adrenaline reside in the flesh you are consuming, creating toxicity in your own body. It also is not uncommon that when the butcher finds cancer in the flesh of the pig, they will simply cut it out and sell the remaining meat to consumers.

Pigs are not picky eaters and will be fed pretty much anything from expired and rotten foods to Halloween candy. Because they do not sweat, they can retain a higher level of toxins which can harm a consumer of pork, both physically and spiritually.

As a general rule, shamans and people practicing certain spiritual traditions do not consume pork at all. Many religions forbid the consumption of pork completely. If you wish to keep your body in a higher energetic and spiritual state, you should consider not consuming pork ever again. Understandably, pork is very much part of our society so even just limiting it following ayahuasca is also another option.

Cow, Veal, Sheep, and Lamb: Abstain 21+ days prior to ceremony

Industrial farming takes a heavy toll on all animals, and this trauma lives in their bodies. As you eat it, all of this goes into your system. Red meat is at the top of the list of foods to avoid prior to consuming ayahuasca as it is a very energetically dense food. When it comes to baby cows (veal) and baby sheep (lamb), it may surprise you to learn that moments after they are born, they are taken from their mothers for slaughter. These mothers and babies have just as strong attachments and yearnings for each other as do humans. This separation and slaughter often occur annually for these mothers and every traumatic event lives in their bodies until they too are slaughtered.

People's opinions regarding meat consumption in many spiritual communities are quite divided. I am not suggesting you give up meat indefinitely and my goal in sharing is not to upset you. I share these grim details because it is important to understand why skipping these foods before consuming this sacred plant medicine is recommended. If you carry the energetic imprinting of animals' traumas, you may have more clean-up work to do during ceremony. Much of the healing with ayahuasca comes through the energy body, so we want to avoid energetic heaviness.

Cured and Processed Meats & Cold Cuts: Abstain 21+ days prior to ceremony

Cured and processed meats and cold cuts are some of the worst processed foods on the market. The World Health Organization classifies most of these foods as a "Group 1 carcinogen"![9] Avoid cold cuts entirely as well as any meat made and processed in a factory. Cured and/or processed meats also have high amounts of tyramine. Avoid pepperoni, bacon, salami, hot dogs, bologna, and smoked fish.

Tuna, Eel & Farm-raised Fish: Abstain 21+ days prior to ceremony

Tuna can have very high levels of mercury, which can cause health complications and at the very least, increase inflammation and toxicity.[10][11] Eel and tuna are also seen by some to be heavy energetic foods, just like red meat.

Farm-raised fish should be avoided as well, for both energetic and physical health reasons. Energetically, farm-raised fish may suffer similarly to farm-raised land animals (depending on the context such as the size and cleanliness of the farm space). Farm-raised fish are often fed unhealthy foods or given supplements that we would not choose to be in our bodies.

Fresh water fish, and ethically sourced organic chicken and eggs in small amounts are often permitted prior to ceremony.

Hard Alcohol and Spirits: Abstain 14+ days prior to ceremony

Ok, this is a tough one, as most people do not want to give up their vino for anything! Asking to abstain for 14+ days may seem outrageous. However, there is a tremendous benefit to omitting alcohol from your diet prior to consuming ayahuasca. Fermented spirits such as beer, vermouth, sherry, and some liqueurs have high amounts of tyramine. Red wine also has high amounts of tyramine as well as tannins, which can upset your gut.

Hard alcohol is actually used by shamans as a tool, but never consumed. Plants are submerged in alcohol to extract its essence and then this is used as medicine. When you get drunk, the body is more susceptible to neighboring entities most of which are of low frequencies. Some say that alcohol can kidnap your spirit!

Up to one week before ceremony, it is okay to consume a six-ounce serving of white wine with food. Feel better now? Good!

Food Categories High in Tyramine: Abstain 14+ days prior to ceremony

As discussed, the following foods that are notoriously high in tyramine should be avoided, as they can make it challenging for your body to process ayahuasca, increasing the chances of a nasty headache, increased blood pressure, or increased nausea.

- Aged cheeses such as cheddar, blue, Swiss, parmesan, feta, Camembert
- Peanuts and peanut butter, Brazil nuts
- All pickled and fermented foods such as sauerkraut, kimchi, pickles, pickled beets, pickled cucumbers, pickled peppers; herring, anchovies
- All fermented soy products such as tofu, tempeh, miso, soy sauce, teriyaki sauce
- Citrus fruits like orange, grapefruit, lemon, lime, tangerine
- Ripe tropical fruits, such as bananas, pineapple, and avocado (higher tyramine levels are present when ripened)
- Dried fruits
- Fermented dairy products such as yogurt, kefir, cultured buttermilk, cottage cheese, sour cream, cream cheese

Other Food Categories: Abstain 14+ days prior to ceremony

Avoid carbonated and fermented drinks (including diet soda, energy drinks, Kombucha, and non-alcoholic beer), industrialized mass-produced food, and all pre-packaged foods that are highly processed and contain high amounts of chemicals and preservatives.

Sex: Abstain 14+ days prior to ceremony

Healing and spiritual growth with ayahuasca are most effective when we maintain sexual purity and a reservoir of sexual energy.

It is not uncommon for shamans to maintain celibacy when doing deep spiritual work or healing within their community. Yogis in India also incorporate celibacy in their spiritual practices as a means to raise consciousness. According to the translated Yoga Sutras of Patanjali, 2.38: *"When firmly established in constant presence of the Divine, sexual continence or chastity, vitality is gained."* In other words, preserved sexual energy can be transmuted and leveraged to reach higher states of consciousness. When this powerful sexual energy is not dissipated, one will have greater strength, vitality and energy and will experience clearer thought and memory.

It is recommended to avoid sexual activity including masturbation two weeks prior to ceremony.

Supplements: Abstain 14+ days prior to ceremony

Many herbal preparations are contraindicated with ayahuasca (recall the above-warning on serotonin-affecting supplements). Avoid the following herbs 14+ days prior to consuming ayahuasca:

Boswellia (Indian frankincense)	Licorice Root
	Nutmeg
Ephedra	Rhodiola Rosea
Ginkgo biloba	Scotch Broom
Ginseng	Sinicuichi
Kanna	St. John's Wort
Kava	Yohimbe
Kratom	

Dairy: Abstain 7+ days prior to ceremony

Back to those poor cows, who not only have their babies taken from them, but are forced to produce even more milk by being fed or injected with growth hormones, insulin, and estrogen. Routine antibiotics are also par for the course, often used due to poor animal husbandry and suboptimal nutrition for the animals.

Over 65% of the world's population has a form of lactose intolerance called lactose malabsorption, which shows up as inflammation or digestive problems.[12] Trust me, you do not want to be gassy in an ayahuasca ceremony! Some believe consuming dairy causes excess mucus as well. Ditch the dairy for as long as possible, but at least for 7 days prior to ceremony. To clarify, dairy is anything made from cow's or goat's milk, including milk, cream, and butter. Fermented dairy products featured above should be avoided 14+ days prior to ceremony.

Spicy Foods: Abstain 7+ days prior to ceremony

Hot and spicy food such as chilies, red pepper, and curry should be avoided prior to your ceremony. Our systems are very sensitive, and spicy foods can cause unnecessary digestive upset and unnecessary turmoil during ceremony. Some shamans also believe intensely-flavored foods can affect the absorption of the medicine.

Coffee: Abstain 7+ days prior to ceremony

Don't shoot the messenger! Coffee is a plant medicine and is said to possibly conflict with ayahuasca. Coffee is also acidic and therefore can cause digestive upset. For these reasons, some tribes and retreat spaces recommend omitting coffee for at least one week prior to consuming ayahuasca.

I have followed this recommendation in the past, and then sometimes not so much. I have even been to retreats where coffee is served. For purposes of the dieta, I make a concerted effort to reduce coffee consumption prior to ceremony. Rather than gulping it down (oh man, it feels so good!), I try to be more mindful when I drink coffee in the days preceding ceremony. You can also add cardamom to your coffee, which may reduce its acidity and neutralize the effects of caffeine.

If you do decide to remove coffee from your diet, and you get the notorious withdrawal headaches, having a little green tea will help. Green tea has roughly 30-50 mgs of caffeine per 8-oz serving, versus coffee which has upwards of 100 mgs of caffeine. Green tea also has antioxidants, which can help with inflammation.

Dark Chocolate: Abstain 7+ days prior to ceremony

Dark chocolate has higher amounts of theobromine compared to milk chocolate, and according to the National Institute of Health's toxicology data network, theobromine crosses the blood-brain barrier, that semi-permeable layer of blood capillaries that allow only certain substances into the brain.[13] The combination of its vasodilation abilities, diuretic effects, and gastrointestinal upset means that, in very high amounts, theobromine can cause a rapid heart rate, loss of appetite, sweating, trembling, and a severe headache. Because of the effects on the cardiovascular system, which include a drop in blood pressure and increased heart rate, theobromine in very high doses can be toxic and fatal. Dark chocolate also contains tryptophan, which is an amino acid that works as a precursor to serotonin, thus increasing serotonin levels.

Salt, Oil, Sugar: Limit / Be mindful

Light consumption of salt is acceptable, but try not to overdo it. If you do need some salt, avoid the cheap processed table salt. Rather find some good quality Himalayan or sea salt, which is less processed than table salt and retains trace minerals.

Avoid highly processed oils like canola oil or vegetable oils. Use good quality avocado oil or coconut oil for cooking and good quality olive oil for very low temp cooking or for salad dressings. Do not heat your oils to a smoking point, as it then becomes harmful for you.

Minimize your consumption of processed sugar as much as possible, especially white sugar. There are many alternatives to sugar that are healthier and more delicious. For example, raw honey, monk fruit sugar, a good quality maple syrup, stevia, agave, coconut nectar, coconut sugar, dates, and molasses are all excellent options. Avoid artificial sugar substitutes entirely for 7+ days.

Dieta Summary - Pre-Ceremony Foods & Activities

30+ Days Prior to Ceremony: All Master Plant Medicines, Hallucinogens (including microdosing) and Street Drugs, including but not limited to:

Cannabis	MDMA
Psilocybin Mushrooms	Crack
Mescaline	Cocaine
Peyote	Heroin
San Pedro	Opioids
Iboga	Methamphetamines
Ketamine	(Crystal/Meth)
LSD	PCP (Angel Dust)

21+ Days Prior to Ceremony:

Pork	Cold Cuts
Cow & Veal	Tuna
Sheep & Lamb	Eel
Cured & Processed Meats	Farm-raised Fish

14+ Days Prior to Ceremony:

Sex, including masturbation
Hard Alcohol & Spirits
Food Categories High in Tyramine, including:

- Aged cheeses
- Peanuts and peanut butter, Brazil nuts
- Pickled and fermented foods
- Fermented dairy products
- Soy products
- Citrus fruits
- Ripe tropical fruits
- Dried fruits
- Carbonated and fermented drinks
- Industrialized and pre-packaged foods
- Supplements

7+ Days Prior to Ceremony:

- Dairy
- Spicy Foods
- Coffee
- Dark Chocolate
- Artificial Sugar
- Salt, Oil, Sugar: Limit / Be mindful

Be aware of how you feel during the dieta and how your body is reacting on an energetic level. Pay attention to your body and honor its cues.

What to Consume

I know I just outlined pretty much every food, drink and activity most people enjoy on a daily basis however, while you are dedicated to the dieta, evaluate how this affects your mental and physical health as well as your spiritual health. This is a good opportunity to make some lasting changes! Some say there is tremendous value to maintaining the dieta for as long as you can before, during, and after consuming ayahuasca.

When it comes to what you actually can eat, it is pretty straight forward. Here are some suggestions:

- Stay hydrated with appropriate amounts of pure spring water throughout the day.
- Consume lots and lots of fruits and vegetables.
- Legumes, beans, and peas are good options and very satiating.
- Don't forget the wonderful whole grains, such as rice, quinoa, buckwheat, barley, as well as cereals including oat, muesli and homemade granola.
- If you are getting full from all this goodness and need to fit in your fruits and veggies, fresh juices are great and hydrating. So are some herbal teas!

(continued...)

- Olive oil and ghee are advised over the other cooking oils, but skip the fried foods altogether.
- Fresh organic eggs are appropriate, but not on the day of ceremony.

Other tips to the dieta:

- If you can get your hands on organic food, that is ideal but not necessary.
- Do your best to keep things low in sodium. The blander, the better.
- Choose natural, whole foods with ingredients that you can pronounce.
- Before you consume, express gratitude to your Higher Power, and all the creatures and people responsible for the food you are eating.
- Practice mindful eating whereas you chew slowly with awareness and experience the healing vibration the food is offering you. Our digestion and bodies benefit when we chew thoroughly and with full attention, tasting the food and appreciating it.

The Dieta After Ayahuasca

You made it. You have consumed ayahuasca and you are a glowing, floating being of light and love. Now let's go grab a burger and a beer. Not!

Now that your ceremony has concluded, it is ideal to maintain the dieta for a period of time. Grandmother Ayahuasca is still with you and will continue to provide you with insights and wisdom over the next several weeks. Maintaining the dieta post-ceremony will not only promote more dialogue with Her, it will allow you to integrate the experience fully.

Among the lessons ayahuasca teaches us, one universal lesson is how to live appropriately in right relationship with ourselves and all else. Though none of us are perfect and that word may not even exist for humans, ideally we will learn from ayahuasca how to eat and otherwise live in ways that are beneficial for our health and awakening processes. In that sense, you may wish over time to adopt more of the general dieta as your normal way of being.

The master shamans of the Amazon remind us that ayahuasca and other plant medicine teachers are spiritual beings with personalities and wisdom to share. If you want to develop a gracious relationship with them, you must demonstrate respect and a commitment in embodying their lessons. Therefore, abstaining from certain habits and foods is also a sign of gratitude and commitment to healing. Such acts do not go unnoticed by ayahuasca and the other healing spirits.

The following post-ayahuasca dieta will help you maintain a healthy connection with the medicine and maximize the benefits of your ceremony during your integration period.

30 Days Following Ceremony - Continue to avoid:
- All master plant medicines, hallucinogens (including microdosing) and street drugs.
- Aged cheeses, especially blue cheese. The fungus and mold in these cheeses can make you physically ill. After 30 days, incorporate little by little.

While cannabis should be avoided for 30 days, CBD oil can be re-introduced in three or four days following your ayahuasca ceremony.

14 Days Following Ceremony - Continue to avoid:
- Alcohol. Getting drunk may sever the energetic connection you have cultivated during ceremony. Your resistance to alcohol will also be significantly reduced following ceremony. After fourteen days of complete sobriety, you may gradually introduce.
- Red meat and pork. If you plan on consuming, introduce gradually and seek out a farmer who raises their livestock in a humane and healthy way.

5 Days Following Ceremony - Continue to avoid:
- Sex (including masturbation)
- Dairy products. A small amount of butter, milk for coffee, yogurt, cream cheese or cottage cheese is OK. Reintegrate yogurt and other dairy products slowly over time.
- Fermented products and soy and soy products
- Spicy foods
- Refined sugar, salts, and oils

Dieta Conclusion

The dieta not only offers each of us the opportunity to have an optimal and safe experience with the medicine, it can actually shine a light on the ways we do not honor our bodies with love and respect. Many people do the dieta in the weeks leading up to ceremony and are surprised to experience emotional and physical withdrawal effects from the substances that were unknowingly ruling their lives. When the automatic knee-jerk reaction to reach for that alcoholic beverage is taken away, for instance, and we are left with discomfort, we then realize we were using these substances to suppress feelings, rather than facing them. This isn't freedom my friend. This is slavery.

A growing trend to continue the dieta forever is not altogether uncommon and it is one of the ways the medicine ultimately improves our lives. The dieta illuminates the wisdom in self-healing and in dealing with the ever shifting nature of feelings and existence. It is for some a very different lifestyle, but you are worth the effort and exploration into a healthier existence.

Chapter 5
Other Preparations for an Ayahuasca Ceremony

There are many wonderful means of preparation you can incorporate in the weeks and months before consuming ayahuasca. While the last chapter primarily outlined what you should or should not consume prior to and following ceremony to prepare your physical body for ceremony, the following practices can prepare your mind and spirit for a successful journey.

Nature

I do not think anyone is going to be surprised to learn that spending time in nature greatly improves your health and wellness. Sadly though, humanity has drifted from their relationship with nature. With life's never-ending list of to-dos, technology, urbanization that cuts people off from their natural surroundings, and the increase of indoor and virtual recreation options, we no longer feel compelled to connect with nature. We have all noticed people sitting at a table with their loved ones or in a beautiful park only to be staring at their phones. I am guilty of this too!

According to several studies, your physical and mental health may suffer with insufficient time in nature. In preparation for your upcoming ceremony, you want to ensure your physical body has the highest vibrational frequency possible and your mind is free and clear of stress.

When most people think of experiencing nature, they envision backpacking through a dense forest with some trekking poles and a bag of granola. While getting fresh air and exercise is highly recommended, you do not have to go outside to experience nature. You are the very embodiment of nature!

Here are some recommendations you can incorporate 21+ days prior to your ayahuasca ceremony:

- Shinrin-yoku (also known as forest bathing) emerged as a term from Japan in the 1980s as a physiological and psychological exercise.[1] It was designed as an eco-antidote to tech-boom burnout and to inspire people to reconnect with and protect the country's forests. Forest bathing is not just a walk in the woods, rather a complete and conscious immersion in nature, allowing the forest or woods to be your medicine. The principles of forest bathing are simply to breathe, relax, wander, touch, listen and heal. To practice Shinrin-yoku, choose a location that will make you feel safe, and allow yourself to drop into all your senses. Bring anything you may need to be comfortable, such as water, snacks, layers of clothing, and perhaps a small blanket to sit on. If you can, leave your phone and digital devices behind, or at the very least, shut them off. Wander aimlessly, allowing your body to take you wherever it wants and remember to use all your senses to appreciate the beauty that surrounds you.

- Watching the beautiful animals right outside your window is a very accessible and easy way to connect with nature. Animals are cute, intelligent, and entertaining. Taking time to watch the squirrels or birds move about their day can help you feel more deeply connected with the world around you. I placed a birdhouse right outside my office window and within a week, I noticed a plethora of brightly colored feathered friends arriving to check out the new food source.

- Air-purifying indoor plants have been all the rage since a 1989 NASA study championed the air-purifying benefits of houseplants.[2] This study revealed that plants have the ability to reduce indoor air pollutants. Indoor plants help boost your mood and productivity, aid in reducing stress, and look pretty awesome too! English Ivy, bamboo, Parlor Palm, Areca Palm and Mother-in-law's tongue (snake plant or St. George's sword) are among the favorite indoor options.

- Outdoor and indoor gardening is a most rewarding nature activity. Going through the process of planting a seed, nourishing it, and watching it grow deepens your connection with nature. It does not even have to be overly complicated: Simply get some seeds (or use the seeds from the fruit you eat), plant them in a small pot, and tend to them daily. As you nourish your plants, enjoy the sunlight on your skin, feel the dirt in your hands and inhale the smell of fertile soil. Be in wonderment at the incredible intelligence of nature as it unfolds right before your eyes.

We are Mother Nature's sons and daughters and connecting with Her does not have to be overly complicated or take too much out of your day. With these techniques, you can start cultivating a meaningful connection with nature and reaping all the physical and mental health benefits that come with it.

In your own time, you can develop and sustain even more ways to connect with nature in a meaningful way.

Breath

Very early on in my ayahuasca experiences, I would suffer terrible panic attacks during ceremony. I almost abandoned the medicine completely, thinking I was not wired for it. However, on some level I knew there was more to explore in this area and I was not ready to walk away. I am a naturally anxious person, so one could argue this experience was not just a part of my ayahuasca journeys, but very much part of my daily life.

Right before a ceremony, I was fortunate to have a conversation with another participant who had experienced the same thing. (You will come to learn, there are no coincidences when it comes to ayahuasca. She is with you, guiding you before, during and after ceremony.) He sat with me for quite some time sharing various breathing exercises. I was hesitant initially; I mean, I have been breathing my whole life. What is this guy going to teach me? But as he started to break down breathing from an anatomical perspective, everything changed!

I can honestly tell you, that night in ceremony, I did have a panic attack. And I can honestly tell you, the breathing techniques he taught me nipped it in the bud quickly. I was able to gain a level of control over my anxiety that I had never experienced before and had one of the most positive experiences to date.

Whether in ceremony or stuck in traffic, breathing mindfully can help anyone deal with anxiety. Learning various breathing techniques and fine tuning them before drinking ayahuasca will improve your chances of using them successfully prior to or in ceremony. I will highlight a few high-level breathing exercises, but if this is something that you would like to explore more fully, there are many books on the subject.

1) Shallow Breathing vs. Deep Breathing

- Shallow Breathing: When we get anxious, we tend to take rapid, shallow breaths that come directly from the chest. This shallow breathing (also referred to as thoracic or chest breathing) can add to the anxiety you are already feeling. Shallow breathing upsets the body's oxygen and carbon dioxide levels, resulting in an increased heart rate, dizziness, muscle tension, and other physical stressors. Because your blood is not being properly oxygenated, this may signal a stress response that contributes to increased anxiety and panic attacks.

- Deep Breathing: Deep breathing (also referred to as diaphragmatic or belly breathing) stimulates the parasympathetic nervous system, which is part of the peripheral nervous system responsible for regulating heartbeat, blood flow, breathing, and digestion. Deep breathing will help calm the body and mitigate the "fight-or-flight" response.

To determine how you are breathing, simply put one hand on your abdomen, above your belly button, and the other hand in the middle of your chest. As you inhale and exhale, notice which hand rises the most. If your aim is deep breathing, the hand on your abdomen should rise and fall the most.

2) Simple Breathing Exercise

The following breathing exercise can be practiced standing up, sitting, or lying down. During these exercises, be mindful of tension in your body and be ready to relax.

- Inhale slowly and deeply through your nose.
    - Aim for a slow count of five, but do the best you can.
    - Try to make your inhale slow; take long sips of air rather than big gulps. Fill your lungs slowly and with control.
    - Your abdomen should expand and your chest should rise very little.

- Exhale slowly through your mouth.
  - Aim for a slow count of eight, but again, do the best you can.
  - As you exhale, scan your body for tension and release. The jaw, shoulders and belly are primary areas where we tend to grip.
  - Some people enjoy making exhales with noise, such as humming, whooshing or shushing. I personally enjoy incorporating sound, but I try to do so quietly so I do not disturb others in ceremony.
  - At the end of your exhale, smile! Several studies find that smiling helps reduce the body's response to stress and lower heart rate in tense situations.

3)   Box Breathing

Box breathing, also known as four-square breathing, may very well be the easiest technique known to man! It is a tried-and-true technique that can work wonders for anxiety and it is easy to learn and practice. To practice box breathing:

- Exhale slowly, releasing all the air from your lungs.
- Inhale slowly through your nose while you count to four in your head. Be aware of how the air fills your lungs.
- Hold your breath for a count of four.
- Exhale slowly for another count of four.
- Hold your breath again for a count of four.
- Repeat this cycle for three to four rounds.

How easy is that? You can combine this technique with deep breathing, making exhales with noise, and of course smiling!

Yoga Asana

It is no secret that yoga asana can make you feel more relaxed. Regardless of your level of expertise, with a regular dedicated practice, yoga can make you feel calmer and more centered. It will increase body awareness, showing you where you are storing tensions and how you are breathing. It will balance your body's subtle energy systems and help manage stress. To add to these benefits, there are several poses that not only can be incorporated into your daily yoga practice, but can also all be done while in ceremony.

Child's Pose (Balasana): This beautiful resting pose can really help restore calmness, regulate breathing, and relax the body.

Kneel on your bed (or next to your bed) and place your sit bones on your heels. Keeping your sit bones on your heels, inhale and raise your arms above your head. Exhale and bend your upper body forward while resting your forehead on the bed. You can put your arms in front of you or lay them next to your body, palms facing up.

Cat (Marjaryasana) and Cow (Bitilasana) Pose: I cannot think of an easier or better way to release tension than this well-known series of yoga movements.

Cat-Cow does a lot, but during ceremony, it opens the chest, encouraging breath to become slow and deep. Coordinating these movements along with proper breathing can relieve stress and calm the mind.

- Start on your hands and knees. Your wrists are directly under your shoulders, and your knees are directly under your hips.
- Place your shins and knees hip-width apart.
- Begin by moving into Cow Pose: Inhale as you drop your belly towards the mat. Lift your chin and chest, and gaze up toward the ceiling.

(continued…)

- Broaden across your shoulder blades and draw your shoulders away from your ears.
- Next, move into Cat Pose: As you exhale, draw your belly to your spine and round your back toward the ceiling. The pose should look like a cat stretching its back.
- Release the crown of your head toward the floor. Do not force your chin to your chest.
- Inhale, coming back into Cow Pose, and then exhale as you return to Cat Pose.

Supine Spinal Twist (Supta Matsyendrasana): This gentle restorative spinal twist is a heart opener and is a great way to stretch, release, and detoxify internal organs.

- Lie on your back, bring your arms out to the sides with the palms face down in a T position. Bend the right knee and place the right foot on the left knee.
- Exhale and drop the right knee over to the left side of your body, twisting the spine and low back. Look at the right finger tips.

- Keep the shoulders flat to the floor, close the eyes, and relax into the posture. Let gravity pull the knee down, so you do not have to use any effort in this posture.
- Repeat on the other side.

Hang out in this posture as long as you feel comfortable and release anything that is not serving you.

Body Scanning

Body scanning is a fundamental practice for healing and it is so easy that everyone can do it!

- Lay down or sit comfortably, either in a cross-legged meditation pose or reclining on a chair or against a wall. Close your eyes.
- Begin by tuning into your inhale and exhale without trying to control it.
- Once you have connected with your breath, it is time to start body scanning. Simply bringing awareness to your feet. Notice how there are sensations that you would not ordinarily be aware of, such as heat, tingling, or perhaps a breeze.

(continued…)

- Continue to scan up your body, inch by inch, searching for sensations. Ankles, calves, knees, thighs, hips, lower abdomen, lower back, upper back, chest, arms, hands, fingers, shoulders, neck, throat, jaw, cheeks, ears, eyes, forehead, top of the head.
- Every place you visit in your body, allow for a release of tension. If you are having difficulty releasing tension, simply breathe into that part of your body with loving kindness.
- There is nothing more you have to do. Just stay present witnessing the experience of your human body, knowing that "Where the mind goes, the energy flows."

You will find that your awareness relaxes your body and mind more and more. This allows your energies to flow, bringing you nourishment, activating the parasympathetic nervous system, and helping the systems of your body to work well. In ceremony with ayahuasca, the benefits of this practice will be 1,000-fold as you help ayahuasca move through your body with less resistance. In this way, you become a partner with Her, an active participant in your own healing.

Visualization

Like body scanning, visualization utilizes the mind's eye in combination with the powerful mindful breathing practice to open huge possibilities for healing.

The simplest and maybe most effective visualization is to envision your breath as white or golden light (you may like to try other colors too). Envision your in-breath as the light, filling your body. As you exhale, envision the breath as light, leaving your body. You can even breathe all the way down to your toes and even deeper into the Earth. Breathe the light energy through you and enjoy as your energy field is magnified.

Here is a practice to help awaken the inner sight: Simply look at a natural scene, like the green grass in your yard, the blue sky, or a purple flower. Now, close your eyes and "remember" the same scene with the same colors. We can all do this and it becomes easier with practice.

Among other visualization exercises, you may like to envision yourself walking in a garden. See the flowers and plants as you walk on a path. Visit with them for a few moments. You may find a large tree in this garden too. Be with this tree, feeling its power and great wisdom and love for you. In these states of visualization, you can ask questions or request blessings from the plants or beings that you meet. Talk to the tree. Ask questions and listen to the answers. You are tapping into your greater intelligent "super-computer" mind.

Visualization meditations have been scientifically proven as very effective in activating healing processes in our bodies. Further, they are helpful in preparing you for your ceremony. Ayahuasca takes us on the inner shamanic journey of the soul. This is largely a visionary experience; you will use your third eye to navigate the realms of your greater being.

House Cleaning

How can I talk about purifying your body and spirit without also discussing your actual physical living environment?

Your physical living environment is quite often a mirror into your inner mind and body. Living in disorganized squalor, in your office, your car, and most certainly in your home and bedroom can reduce your vibration, add to everyday stress, cause anxiety, and even interfere with your quality of sleep. Ask yourself these questions: What does my current environment say about me? Are there ways I can easily improve the energy of my physical environment? Do I deserve a beautiful, clean, organized environment?

During an ayahuasca ceremony, you will be working on your inner environment, so consider improving your physical environment beforehand as a means to raise your vibration, and begin a dialog with Her. Do a preparatory purge of your physical environment. Your home is your sacred space and you deserve to live in beautiful, clean surroundings. Dedicate this time to yourself to create a living environment that leaves you feeling calm, happy, and well-rested.

If you are overwhelmed by this task, start by first making a list of priorities. You do not need to complete every item on this list in a day, but getting organized will make you feel more in control and able to tackle the tasks at hand. I personally start with the smaller to-dos, and find that the momentum naturally takes me onto the bigger tasks with greater ease. If your physical environment has become way too overwhelming, there are professionals that specialize in space clearing who can help you get organized.

As mom would say, "Clean your damn room!" And feel so much happier!

Conclusion: Other Preparations for an Ayahuasca Ceremony

The goal in these practices is not only spiritual awareness, it is self-awareness. We are often mindlessly running the rat race, and we forget to slow down and enjoy the present moment. Being in nature, discovering breathing and yoga techniques, body scanning, visualization and cleaning your home are great ways to connect to the inner flow of your wisdom and healing.

Chapter 6
The Power of Intentions & How to Create Effective Ones

Ayahuasca is a powerful plant medicine teacher offering an opportunity to not only heal, but to learn. With proper planning and preparation, that opportunity increases tenfold. This is where intentions come in.

All creation begins with intentions, and they are the framework for any spiritual endeavor. Putting thought into your purpose for drinking ayahuasca ahead of time is a valuable part of your preparation and sets you up for the best outcome. Let's face it, the reason you are doing the work is as important as the work itself, if not more so! When we consume the medicine, we are gaining access to Universal intelligence. Be prepared, for example, with the questions you want answered, for the encounters you want to have, or for the healings you wish to achieve. Your intention, if clearly understood and centrally held, can help keep you anchored during ceremony. It will be your reference point throughout ceremony and will help ground you if the experience gets overwhelming.

Coming up with an intention can be challenging. You can come to ayahuasca with one intention or many. I have discovered I am not the only one with a very long list of things I want to learn and heal from. To hone in on an intention, you have to really understand what truly matters to you and it requires self-reflection and an audit of your life. You will find that the process of clarifying your intention is indeed very much part of the healing journey.

When working with ayahuasca, the aim is to identify, clear, and transform trapped energies that hold us back, cause emotional distress, and create perpetual discomfort and disease. Surrendering to the medicine will require tremendous effort and a bit of faith on your part, but it is essential to cleansing and integrating painful memories, deeply embedded emotional blockages, energetic imprints, and self-limiting patterns. Do you desire a life filled with joy, abundance, and inner peace? I certainly do! Now, let's consider how to work with that intention for wellbeing.

How Do I Create an Effective Intention?

Taking adequate time to discover your truest intentions is ideal. Carve out time to really contemplate how you wish to improve your life by drinking the medicine. Consider what success following the experience looks like to you. Reflect, journal, walk, sit with yourself, meditate, ask questions and listen to the answers that arise.

The foundation to develop the best intention is to start with the basics. The following initial questions are important to ponder. Having clarity on these questions will help guide your decision to drink ayahuasca as well as determine your desired intentions.

1. Why have I decided to work with ayahuasca?

2. What do I expect to happen during ceremony?

3. What don't I want to happen during ceremony?

4. Do I feel I have been called to drink ayahuasca? Why or why not?

5. Am I making the decision to drink ayahuasca free and clear of any outside influence?

(continued...)

6. What is my current mindset?

7. What have I done to prepare myself physically?

8. What have I done to prepare myself mentally?

9. What have I done to prepare myself spiritually?

10. Is there something I would like to change in my life?

11. What would I not like to not change following my experience?

12. How will my beliefs affect or influence my experience?

13. Are there opportunities to come to the medicine with a more open heart and mind?

14. What do I consider a good outcome to consuming ayahuasca?

15. Am I having doubts or concerns? If yes, are there preparations I can make to alleviate these doubts or concerns?

Once you have a clearer perspective on why you are consuming ayahuasca, you can contemplate your intentions. The following questions are simply thought starters, but it will give you an idea of what others have focused on. One may jump out at you, or they may all miss the mark. This is a very personal aspect of preparation, so take your time.

1. Why am I the way I am?

2. Am I knowingly or unknowingly holding resentment, grudges?

3. How do I discover and express my authentic self?

4. What burden am I carrying that is causing me pain?

5. Can I remove negative behaviors or thought patterns about myself?

6. Why am I addicted to <alcohol, cigarettes, drugs, etc.>? Show me how to remove <addiction> from my life.

7. Are there addictions in my life that I am not aware of?

(continued…)

8. How do I forgive myself?

9. What is my life's work?

10. What is the highest version of myself?

11. How do I let go of <fear, anger, shame, resentment, the past, etc.>?

12. What is the nature of reality?

13. What is the meaning of life?

14. How do I heal my chakra(s)?

15. Where does this <physical illness> stem from? How can I heal it?

16. How do I surrender to the medicine?

17. How do I develop a balanced ego that knows how to give and receive love?

18. What is blocking me from receiving <wealth, love, health, etc.>?

19. Will You show me the matrix?

20. How is everything connected?

21. How can I be open and willing to learn what You want to show me?

If you are feeling especially stumped, do not fear. You can always write a letter to Grandmother Ayahuasca. What would you like to tell Her? What would you like to ask Her? Sometimes opening up a dialog with Her can help guide your truest needs and desires.

One last important mention on intentions: Ayahuasca may or may not address your intentions immediately. I have gone into a ceremony with a specific intention, only to be taught a very different lesson entirely. Do not be disappointed! Ayahuasca is a master plant medicine teacher and She knows exactly how to work with you. She will work on priorities first, and perhaps get to your wish list at a later time. I know this is frustrating for some, but She absolutely knows what She is doing. Take comfort in surrendering to the process and know that She is doing what is for your highest good.

Intentions vs. Expectations

It is likely you have read or heard of people's life-changing experiences after an ayahuasca ceremony. When I began my journey with plant medicine, I would use their experiences as a gauge of sorts, and if my journey fell short of unicorns and rainbows, I was disappointed or thought I was perhaps doing it wrong. (You cannot do it wrong, by the way. It is impossible!)

The truth is, going in with expectations makes it incredibly challenging to be open to Her path and your own unique experience. I have been in many ceremonies where the only experience was purging. At the time, I would feel very disappointed, especially sitting next to someone who was raving about their conversation with God and how they now know the reason they were born! Talk about a stark difference. That dude was sitting right next to me? Why was I puking all night and he was sitting there having a chit chat with our Creator?!?

The saying goes, "Ayahuasca will give you what you need, not what you want," and that could not be a truer statement. Having complete trust in Her and surrendering to what She knows is an important aspect to having the best experience and outcome. Releasing expectation takes awareness and can feel challenging, but this is a powerful exercise not only in ceremony, but in life. Isn't expectation, or attachment as the Buddha would say, the root of all suffering?

Every single ceremony you participate in (and every single cup during one ceremony!) may be different. Every time you drink you heal, release, learn, and grow. When you are at the other side of that ceremony, you emerge a different person. The next time you arrive in ceremony, you are a completely different human with different needs and a different set of priorities.

If you decide to drink ayahuasca more than once, you may notice some ceremonies will absolutely blow your mind. Other ceremonies you may feel bored or actually sleep through! It does not matter how much you drink or what your understanding of the outcome was. She is in charge and there's no telling what She will do or where She will take you.

Intention as Cosmogenesis

It is worth reiterating that your intention is as important as the medicine itself. One core lesson to learn through ayahuasca is that each of us is the creator of our realities. In this age of awakening, the Western mind is beginning to incorporate the concept of "manifesting" through helpful paths such as Rhonda Byrne's book, *The Secret* or Dr. Joe Dispenza's book, *Becoming Supernatural*. However we define it, whether as spiritual or quantum physics, some theorize the Universe is forming itself based on our beliefs, perceptions, wishes, desires, and clarity of intention.

While I am a strong advocate for trusting the visions from the medicine, you can also practice your powers of manifestation through intention, prayer, and visualization. Go ahead and write down something you want to experience, such as unexpected income coming to you. You can pray for this money to come and visualize the experience of it happening. Feel how it is to receive this extra moolah, the joy, the gratitude, and the wonderment in seeing your wish come true. If you set intentions with your heart glowing and softly burning with desire, then it is more likely to happen.

With ayahuasca, you have the opportunity to manifest your wishes more powerfully because She is removing things that no longer serve you and clearing the channels of your energy field. It is like upgrading to a super-high speed internet system! Your life vision, hopes, dreams, and prayers can be made clear instantly by the "super-computer" of the Great Cosmic Mind.

The mirror metaphor is another way to look at manifestation: The content of your mind is reflected back to you in the material world. Your ayahuasca journey is about cleaning the mirror so that you may live a full creative life.

When drinking the medicine, consider creating your intention based on a more generalized prayer of your highest wellbeing. Most of us come to ceremony searching for a higher expression of ourselves to be lived in the world. We each want to live to our full potential, offering the unique gifts of our soul at the highest level of cultivation. Rather than asking ayahuasca for riches and luxury, intentions based on healing, truth, love, highest purpose, and service may indeed be the most meaningful and effective.

Intentionally Concluding

Pay special attention to cultivating your intention before sitting with ayahuasca, as this experience can be pivotal for your health and life journey. Ultimately, your intention for healing and the vision for your future life is yours and yours alone. No one can tell you what to want, but remember that honing in on your intentions can influence what you experience in ceremony.

If you are seeking to know who you are and what the nature of God is, you may find yourself in one powerful spiritual journey. Some spiritual paths are entirely based on asking questions like, "Who am I?" because this question itself activates the spiritual process of awakening. However, if you decide to show up with less cosmic endeavors and are more of a curious mind, well that is great too, but you may have a wholly different experience. Ultimately, your intention and prayer most often determine what happens in ceremony, as well as in life.

Historically, Amazonian tribes were the only ones blessed to commune with ayahuasca. Now you have an opportunity to commune with Her as well. Anytime you bow to Her altar and receive the medicine in your body, you are in the presence of a great master. Drop all attachments and expectations and receive the medicine with gratitude. Do not squander the opportunity. Be prepared with clear intentions.

Chapter 7
What to Expect in Ceremony

At the center, the shaman.

The shaman is most certainly the presider for this transcendent group experience, some of whose participants are first timers, others who are embarking on their hundredth ceremony. The shaman is indeed one of the most important aspects of an ayahuasca ceremony, and without one, things can go very wrong. Not only are the shamans experienced healers, but they will bless the medicine with intention, and clear and protect the ceremony space and everyone who participates, ensuring no demon ne'er-do-wells creep into our lives.

Would you trek deep into the jungle without the help of a trained professional? Of course not! Journeying into multi-dimensional or spiritual spaces is unfamiliar and scary at times and it is necessary to have someone lead you through unknown terrain.

With an experienced shaman serving the medicine, holding the space, and guiding the ceremony, you as the participant may relax fully into your ayahuasca journey knowing that you do not have to do anything and that you are in safe hands. Do your research on who the shaman is, their experience, and their lineage ahead of time so you can just show up and trust the process.

The Ceremony Basics

Ayahuasca ceremonies are typically held at sundown in a large circular hut called a maloca. Ceremonies are usually in a group setting ranging from five to twenty-five people, but I have seen upwards of eighty to one-hundred participants in one night. Most retreat centers offer several nights of ceremony in a row to help reduce resistance to the medicine and allow for a deeper immersion. Every night that you consume the medicine, the reaction and results will likely be very different, because with every ceremony, you emerge as a different person.

On the day of ceremony, it is best to eat very little, stopping completely within a five-hour to eight-hour window of drinking ayahuasca. Undigested food may impede the absorption of the medicine and can make you nauseous. Water and clear juices are acceptable throughout the day, but try to limit yourself within a one-hour window of drinking ayahuasca.

Before ayahuasca is served, the space is prepared and blessed by the shaman leading the ceremony. The shaman and facilitators will likely smudge each participant with cleansing herbs like white copal, palo santo or sage. You may receive Agua de Florida (Florida Water, or "Water of the Flowers"; see Definitions) in the palms of your hands to smell and apply to the top of your head, and your face, neck, arms and chest. Some shamans may sip the Agua de Florida in their mouth and, with intention, spit-spray it onto your energetic field, including your head and body, front and back. This is called Soplar or Sopla, which means "to blow " and is used by the shaman to transfer or clear energy. The shaman may ask you to lift your shirt and/or expose as much skin as comfortably as possible. It is ideal to get optimal coverage of the Agua de Florida onto your skin.

There are typically numerous experienced facilitators who assist during ayahuasca ceremonies. Get to know their names before the ceremony begins. They will monitor everyone's safety and address your needs throughout the night. They are there to support you, so do not be afraid to request help or ask questions. They will get you a blanket if you are cold, walk you to the bathroom if you are unsteady, and sit with you if you are scared. They are our salves and the literal embodiments of angels. They are an essential part of ceremony and I cannot sing their praises enough.

If you are attending an ayahuasca ceremony with your spouse, child, sibling, bestie, or anyone you are close with, make sure you are as far away from them as humanly possible. It can be incredibly challenging to drop into your own journey if you are listening to someone you love going through a process. Your energy can also co-mingle with theirs making it especially challenging for you both, so it is best to separate.

Most ceremonies request participants take a vow of silence before the medicine is served. This gives everyone an opportunity to settle into their space, contemplate their intentions, meditate and do some deep breathing. It is a great opportunity to cultivate the optimal mindset.

Some Pointers

- It is completely normal and very common to be nervous before ceremony. However, if you are exceptionally nervous, try to improve your mindset prior to consuming the medicine with some simple practices such as prayer, journaling, talking to others before entering the ceremony space, breathing exercises, and stretches. Your mindset can affect your journey.

- Typically, you will begin by consuming a shot sized glass of ayahuasca at room temperature. If you are new to the medicine, start with a low dose. Everyone reacts differently to ayahuasca and there is no harm in going slowly.

- When the shaman feels the group is ready for more medicine, typically within an hour or two following the initial dose, she or he will call for a second glass.
  - If you are not feeling the effects of the medicine, drink more.
  - If you are feeling the effects of the medicine, drink more.

The point is, as long as you can get up, walk to the shaman and request more medicine, try to do so. Drink more, especially if the shaman calls upon you specifically.

- Some centers encourage or at least allow you to request more medicine following the second cup until you are satisfied with the depth of your journey. If this applies to you, wait at least 45 minutes after your last dose before drinking more.

Immediately after drinking ayahuasca, it is advised to return to your cot and sit in an upright position with your spine erect for as long as possible and no less than 30 minutes. Keeping your spine straight helps the medicine flow through your whole body more efficiently, thus reducing nausea. You may prefer to sit on the edge of a cushion so your knees are below your hips to release tension in your lower back. You can also bring a meditation chair with a back to lean on.

Aside from shamanic chanting and possibly the occasional check-in from facilitators, the space is silent. Once the medicine is served, everyone observes a vow of silence and there is certainly no touching, gesturing, or helping of others who are consuming. In ceremony, you will be open on many levels of your being. You and everyone else will be in vulnerable and suggestive states where energies are easily transferable. All ceremonies require you to maintain your boundaries and respect those of all others too.

One thing that took me by surprise is that most of the time, the shamans and facilitators drink as well. I bring this up because from an outside perspective, one may think this is creating an unsafe environment. Aren't these people here to help and support me? How can they do that if they are on the medicine? The truth is they must drink ayahuasca so they can drop into the same space you are in. They need access to the spirit world to help guide those in need of help. Do not worry; They typically have a support system in place for each other. Also, facilitators usually drink what is called a "facilitator's dose," which is half of your initial dose. Facilitators are generally not in deep personal journeys.

After consuming ayahuasca, most people start to feel its effects within an hour. The intensity and length of your journey are variable based on the strength of the medicine, the dose and frequency of doses. Your whole journey is estimated to last on average for four hours and can range from two to eight hours. An ayahuasca ceremony from the first cup to feeling sober and able to go back to your room varies. The ceremony concludes once the shaman sees the effects have worn off in the collective group. In most ceremonial spaces, you are welcome to sleep the rest of the night right on your ceremonial mat. You may like to enjoy the soft afterglow of ceremony and resting within the protection of the altar, so bring your bedding just in case.

It is important to know, there are usually a handful of people in every ceremony who have an intense experience. By that I mean they have an all-out powerful episode, or series of episodes that everyone in the maloca (and sometimes beyond) can hear and feel. I have seen people scream at the top of their lungs, curse, thrash, make a run for it, growl and crawl around like animals, and the like. The first time I experienced this, I became incredibly upset and emotional, but I am here to tell you, don't. I know it can be difficult to witness people seemingly go through the worst experience of their lives and it may be hard to wrap your head around this, but what is happening is actually incredibly deep healing. Many people come to ayahuasca with deep trauma, and this is the process of releasing it. It is natural. It is acceptable. It is nothing to be ashamed of. Everyone in the room supports each other. The maloca is totally protected and is a safe space to release. If you are hearing someone having an intense experience, pray for them, and surround them with love and light. Then, do your best to drop back into your own journey. Do not spend too much time getting attached to someone else's experience. You have your own work to do!

Deconstruction of a Ceremony, Step by Step

1. Participants arrive to the ceremony space, set-up their beds/mats, and settle in.
   - Pro tip: When drinking ayahuasca in a larger facility, try to sit closer to the medicine and/or the altar because the vibration is higher there.
   - Be Aware: If there is live music and you are sensitive to it, sit further away and consider having ear plugs ready to help mute it.
   - Suggestion: If you are like me and pretty much have to pee every half hour, sit closer to the bathroom. It is just easier!
2. The shaman arrives, may have a conversation with the group, blesses the medicine.
3. Participants receive their energetic cleansing via white copal, palo santo, sage or Agua de Florida (may happen before or after the shaman arrives).
4. People are called to take their first drink, at which point they will line up and drink, typically one at a time.
5. Within 30-45 minutes, hearing purging activity is common.
6. Within 1 to 2 hours, the shaman will call for a second cup.
7. Within 4-6 hours from the first drink, the shaman will close the ceremony.

While this step-by-step guide will help you mentally prepare for your ceremony, ceremonies led by shamans of different traditions may vary considerably. Although ceremonies are generally in the evening and in complete darkness, there is usually low lighting so you can walk around if need be.

Lastly, I offer you this Protection Prayer, which may help you connect with the Grandmother before ceremony:

Thank you, dear Grandmother, for blessing me with this sacred medicine. I come to you for healing, wisdom, love, and safety and I am eternally grateful for Your presence. Help me to connect with You more deeply, communicate with You more effectively, and surrender to You more completely. Your love and goodness surround me on this day and I do not fear. Guide me on my journey and protect me every step of the way.

Music in Ceremony

Ayahuasca icaros (or ikaros) are traditional indigenous Amazonian songs that are performed by the shaman as an accompaniment to the sacred plant medicine.[1] Icaros are musical prayers that invoke specific shamanic powers and embody the powers of the plant spirits, animals, deities, ancestors, and elemental forces. Channeled into the ceremony by the shaman, they are healing agents, powerful spirit weapons, and ineffable realm creators. Icaros can include singing, instrumental music with harmonica, flute, jaw-harp and other instruments, purging sounds, whistling, and speaking in tongues.

Shamans often learn icaros through years of training, extensive dietas (discussed in Chapter 4), and communing with the plant medicine teachers.[2] The shamanic dieta is more rigorous and devotional than a participant's expected preparation and is necessary for the shaman to receive the icaros from the plants and spirits. Shamans may also be taught these sacred melodies by their elders, as they are passed down through generations of healers. Because of their origins, icaros are often sung in Quichua or Spanish.

A ceremony may also feature musicians who sing and play their instruments on and off throughout the night. I recall after a particularly long night, the musician softly played Blackbird by the Beatles. It was so incredibly moving and soothing that I sat up and started to cry in gratitude. That is a moment in time that I will never forget. When music is part of the ceremony, the vibrations of voice and instruments are often intentionally and carefully selected to open you up for deeper healing.

There are times when ceremonies are in complete silence for the majority of the night, allowing for intense inner-focus from each participant. If you work with ayahuasca more frequently, you will find the tradition that most speaks to your heart.

Limpias

The shaman may perform a cleansing ritual on you known as a limpia, which is a very powerful and important part of the ceremony. Limpias can be performed during or after an ayahuasca ceremony. I was once told by a shaman that limpias are more effective when the recipient is very deep in the medicine.

Limpias are typically performed one-on-one with the shaman and the recipient. A limpia may include any or all of the following:

- Rhythmic shaking of the chacapa leaves onto the head, back, and body.
- Icaros and/or chanting, which can support the process of cleansing, healing, purging, balance energy, calm the mind, offer strength and protection, take the recipient on a spiritual journey, invoke helping spirits and banish negative energies.

- Plant extracts such as Agua de Florida (Florida Water) can be poured into your hands to breathe in or apply to the top of your head, and your body. It may also be applied by the shaman via soplar.
- Use of mapacho smoke blown over and around your body, front and back.
- Playing of various instruments.

You may have the opportunity to request a limpia, especially if you come to ceremony with an illness or injury. While not every shaman performs limpias on the participants individually, talk to a facilitator prior to ceremony to determine what is available for your healing journey.

What to Wear

What you decide to wear to an ayahuasca ceremony is a personal choice and may largely depend on where you are consuming the medicine. Keep in mind, this is a beautiful ceremony and an opportunity to commune with the Divine. It is a celebration! As such, many people choose to wear white or bright colors, and some retreat centers even request it. Most people would not go to a celebration in sweatpants, right? It may be best to check in with your facilitator to get their input.

The most important advice is to wear clothing that is comfortable and loose fitting. There is nothing worse than being on the medicine, needing to purge, and having to fiddle with a belt buckle or a button fly. I also do not recommend clothes that will drag on the floor when you are in the bathroom.

Shoes are often not permitted to be worn inside the ceremonial space. If you prefer not to be barefoot, consider wearing socks with grips on the bottom. Depending on where I am consuming, sometimes I am able to leave a pair of flip flops near the bathroom entrance, for obvious reasons.

You may choose to wear some sacramental or power accessories as well. Many people believe that wearing certain types of jewelry can protect and ground them, and have a positive effect on their journey. Just remember, be comfortable and do not wear jewelry that is too restrictive or likely to get in the way.

Some participants like to connect with the spirit of ayahuasca by bringing or wearing items symbolically inspired by the medicine. Symbols such as jaguars and other felines, snakes, birds, otherworldly beings, cities, palaces, divine beings, jungles and forests, and kaleidoscope patterns are all very common.

Crystals & Gemstones

Popular spiritual tools such as crystals and gemstones are not only revered for their powerful, healing energies, but are believed to offer many benefits. Here is just a short list of some accoutrements you may consider bringing or wearing:[3]

- Aquamarine: Protects and brings luck, dispels nerves, and provides calm, self-love, and acceptance.
- Amethyst: Healing, purifying, and enhancing willpower; purifies the mind and facilitates connection to the divine.
- Bloodstone: Boosts strength, courage, and resilience; Helps you feel safe; Clears and transmutes negative energy.
- Citrine: Cultivates energy and fertility for growth; helps radiate power, confidence, and endurance and clears negative energy.
- Clear quartz: Supports the entire energetic system; considered by some to be a master healer.
- Emerald: Connects to the Heart Chakra and enhances intuition and psychic abilities. Brings awareness of the unknown to conscious recognition, imparting reason and wisdom.
- Hematite: Offers healing and protection against evil, and grounds an individual.

(continued…)

- Jasper: Nurturing; provides support during times of stress.
- Moonstone: Promotes feelings of inner strength and growth.
- Obsidian: Helps process emotions and experiences; aids in letting go.
- Pearl: Promotes integrity, truth, purity, charity, and loyalty.
- Rose Quartz: Encourages love and trust; stone of love.
- Ruby: Aids in emotional wellbeing, increases integrity, devotion, and happiness.
- Sapphire: Helps achieve inner peace, aids in meditation, and promotes creative expression.
- Tiger's Eye: Provides motivation and lessens fear.
- Topaz: Protects against greed and facilitates the balance of emotions.
- Turquoise: Soothes emotions and attracts good luck; healing and balancing.

What to Bring

Generally speaking, most ayahuasca retreat centers will provide everything you need during the ceremony. Ideally, you will be provided a mattress, a pillow, a blanket, a bucket in which you can vomit, if necessary, and tissues. Beyond that, here are some things you may want to consider bringing to ceremony:

- A water bottle: Although it is recommended you do not drink water at all during the ceremony, I have water available in the event I want to swish my mouth out following a purge. Once ceremony is closed, you can drink water slowly.

- A small flashlight: Ceremony space is typically dimly lit and if you have to find your way to the bathroom, it is a huge help. A red light flashlight is ideal, as it helps to preserve night vision and decrease the overall light signature in low-light situations. Red light does not cause the human eye pupil to shrink to the same degree as more bluish/white light.

(continued...)

- A change of clothes: A lot can go down (and come up!) during an ayahuasca ceremony and you may feel more comfortable if you have back up clothing. Bringing layers of clothing is also recommended, as you may get hot or cold throughout the night.

- An eye mask: If you are particularly sensitive to light, an eye mask may come in handy. While the maloca is usually quite dark, sometimes facilitators and other participants use their flashlight to walk around and it could disturb your journey.

- Earbuds: The ceremony space can get loud, between people going through their processes and music, so bring earbuds if you are sensitive to noise and get easily distracted.

- Insect repellant: If you are consuming ayahuasca in the jungle, I highly recommend protecting yourself from mosquitos. Natural repellents containing both citronella and eucalyptus oil work well.

- Hair ties: For those with long hair, it may feel more comfortable to have your hair tied back. I do not recommend hard hair clips that may hurt your head while lying down.

- An altar / specialty items: Some people like to bring a favorite crystal, or an item that has meaning to them. This can help ground a participant during a challenging journey.

- A journal and pens: A lot of information can come through during an ayahuasca ceremony, so having a journal handy may be useful to jot down notes. It is unlikely you will be writing during ceremony, but shortly thereafter, it may be more convenient to document details of your journey.

Do not bring a cell phone, a smart watch, or anything digital. This energetic work is very sensitive to bright lights and anything with strong electromagnetic frequencies. You can survive without these devices for one evening and it will enable you to stay focused on yourself. You also do not want to call your mom in the depths of the night while you are still processing, telling her how much you love her and that you now know she did her best. You will scare her!

Final Ceremony Pointers

There you have it! That is all you need to know about the ceremony format. If you come prepared with the right materials to be comfortable, then you can simply relax and have a wonderful ceremony.

When you arrive to the ceremony, you are immediately entering sacred space. The ceremonial room with the altar is to be treated with reverence. That does not mean you should be nervous, but rather that you may conduct yourself with careful intention. When you have arrived in the temple of the Goddess, remember where you are. Know that She is already there, watching over everyone with love and wisdom. Proceed with an honorable and dignified posture and feel free to be happy!

Chapter 8
What Am I Going to Feel

> *in·ef·fa·ble*
> /inˈefəb(ə)l/
> adjective
> too great or extreme to be expressed or described in words.

The number one question participants ask prior to an ayahuasca experience is "What am I going to feel?" The trouble is, when it comes to this mystical medicine, putting into words how ayahuasca will feel can be incredibly challenging. I promised in the Introduction that I was not going to talk in fancy mystical terms, and I will do my best to keep that promise. However, things are about to get pretty weird!

Let us start with the basics. Everyone's experience with ayahuasca can vary tremendously. To add to that, if you participate in more than one ceremony, every personal experience you have can vary tremendously. While your experience of ayahuasca is highly individual, and will be different for every person in a ceremony, there are some benchmark experiences that I would like to share. I have included my first hand and other participant's second-hand accounts of their journeys as well.

While it is super important to go into ceremony without any assumptions or expectations, many people want to have some point of reference for their experience and I understand that. However, please keep in mind what I am sharing is just that: a point of reference. Everything I am about to share may be completely irrelevant for you personally.

There are several ways you may experience the medicine. You can have a **physical journey**, a **visionary journey**, a **consult**, or a combination of some or all three of the journeys. Alternatively, you can experience **absolutely nothing**.

I have noticed people are usually pretty nervous before drinking ayahuasca because of a combination of two contrary things: They do not know what to expect, and they have expectations! Regardless, it is completely reasonable to feel anxiety or nervousness before consuming this sacred medicine. First timers do not know what to expect. Neither do people who have drunk one-hundred times. We really never know how the experience will unfold and what it will bring. While this unknowingness requires nerves of steel, it also keeps it fresh, new, and exciting.

Pretty quickly after you consume the medicine, you may experience an unusual sensation in your stomach, some heat in the body, and perhaps some mild nausea. Breathe into these initial physical sensations and be patient as they generally pass within thirty minutes. If you start to read too much into these initial sensations and attach to them, you may induce unnecessary worry and anxiety.

Within thirty to sixty minutes, as the medicine continues to spread through your body, you may start to notice a change in perception and thought patterns. On average, the full effect of ayahuasca will come on in about one hour, but it may start within thirty minutes or even take one and a half to two hours before it reaches maximum intensity. It depends on your metabolism and really, Her.

Whatever comes up, try not to overthink what you are experiencing, rather lean toward the messages, visions, emotions, and physical sensations, even if they are very uncomfortable, frightening or do not make sense.

If you do find yourself really uncomfortable or anxious, there are several options to consider:

- Your breath is your life. It is everything and can help calm you down, so breathe deeply into the space where the discomfort lies. I recommend revisiting and practicing some of the breathing techniques offered in Chapter 5.

- Body scanning is my go-to when I am having a tough moment. I am always able to find areas in my body that are gripping and tense. Breathing into and releasing that tension can make a world of difference.

- Connect with authentic gratitude to Her for the experience you are having. Although you may feel uncomfortable, know that everything that is happening is for your greater good and you are blessed.

- Shift your focus to your intentions and the reason you have consumed the medicine. Remember your higher self is being called to heal.

- Ask Her questions and instead of resisting the discomfort, lean into it with curiosity. Perhaps this discomfort is something you have knowingly or unknowingly been dealing with your whole life.

- Remind yourself that you are completely safe. The sensations you are feeling are the medicine at work, and you are in a process of healing.

- You can always ask ayahuasca for help or to receive the teaching in another way, but know that if She does not honor that request, She knows you can handle what is happening. We often do not know how strong we are until we are faced with challenges and persevere.

- Pray to God/Creator/Source.

- When all else fails, ask for help from the support staff. They often have tools at their disposal that can help you move through the experience quicker. Sometimes just knowing someone is there who cares for you is enough to make you feel more comfortable and at peace.

So, what will you feel and experience during your ayahuasca journey? A similar question can be asked about what you will feel and experience during your entire lifespan starting with the intensity and trauma of birth, the boundless joy of seeing the world for the first time, and tasting the fruits of Gaia. Feeling the immense intoxication of your first love and the subsequent plummet into despair over your first broken heart. Laughing so hard that you cannot breathe, and then, at times, crying even harder. Your precious life's experiences may never cease to amaze you, playing all the notes of your soul until the coda of your death, which you will also experience. So, on an ayahuasca journey, expect to feel. You signed up for this human adventure so you may as well cash in on your birthright. Feel it all, baby!

Physical Journey

A physical journey is predominantly defined by purging. The range of physical experiences that may occur as a purge is so broad that the entire Chapter 9 in this book outlines only some of the possibilities. Many shamans believe when you consume ayahuasca two or more nights in a row, then it is likely you will spend the first night experiencing deep physical and energetic clearing which will enable a deeper visionary and spiritual journey the subsequent nights. I have found this to be true for most participants.

Healers, meditators, and yogis who practice embodiment may place high value on the physical journey of ayahuasca. While some people may rave about their third eye visions, just as valuable—if not more so—is the journey into the meat and bones of the body. The body is a storehouse of the unresolved emotions and memories from our entire lives. Ideally, if you are coming to ayahuasca for healing rather than a psychedelic joyride, you will benefit by releasing the energetic blocks that are tied to repressed memories and emotions.

Delving deeply into the body, feeling into sore places, allowing old wounds to surface, and waiting patiently for the knots to loosen may be a painful experience but it is supremely worthwhile. The physical journey is how you open up to yourself and accept all your parts, even the ones that are ashamed, angry, afraid, and bitter about the past.

Breath is the key here.

I will say this several times throughout the book because it is a top priority. By breathing into discomfort and pain, you can return your full awareness to your repressed self.

As you experience the physical journey, no matter what is coming up, you may find your body more and more enlivened with energy flowing through your channels and chakras. The dark and painful terrain of your shadow can in one moment become the portal to heaven. The "curse" becomes the "blessing". Out of the darkness comes light. On a physical journey, you may find yourself swinging from blissful sensations to torment and back again. Regardless, always maintain unconditional, accepting awareness, just like in mindfulness meditation.

Beyond purging, a physical journey can take many shapes. Sacred surgery and ego death are two of the more profound experiences which are both truly ineffable. Whatever you experience during your physical journey, no matter how uncomfortable, it is part of the healing and cleansing process that ayahuasca is masterfully helping you through. There are a million lessons that ayahuasca may be teaching you, but the way forward is always just to stay present and connected to your heart, accepting whatever is happening. Trust Her. Trust the process.

Sacred Surgery

It is not uncommon for people to report spiritual or energetic forms of surgery or operations during ceremony. *Um, what? That's pretty far out, right? Surely, the result of a hallucination?* Actually, receiving a sacred surgery is not uncommon during an ayahuasca ceremony.

Sacred surgery may start with seeing in one's third eye celestial surgeons, described as beings from another space and time. Terence McKenna most famously referred to these beings as the Machine Elves, who sing in a hyper-dimensional language and welcome you warmly! Some report these celestial surgeons looking humanoid, or like insects. (The praying mantis is quite popular.) I have even heard a participant share that these celestial surgeons look like minions. The being may ask for permission to address physical issues, or may just get to work. You may feel energy, electricity, pulling, poking, and other physical sensations throughout your body. One participant shared, "I felt that my heart was open and they were healing it."

Whoever these beings are, they sometimes enter our personal space and offer us healing, downloads of information, or energetic upgrades. For instance, the following is not an uncommon thing to hear someone share following a ceremony during an integration circle: "Last night I experienced an insectoid flying into my chest. It buzzed and sent waves of warmth through my heart. I knew it was giving me a gift." Indeed, such other-dimensional beings can perform surgery on old physical or psychic wounds and even put spiritual implants in your body. There are often reports of people receiving sacred surgeries and not only feeling sore in the days and weeks following their ceremony, but being completely cured of the illness they came to the ceremony with!

When you shift into ayahuasca-consciousness, you are likely to become aware of yourself as a multi-dimensional being. In our normal waking consciousness, we may experience ourselves as physical beings, with mental or psychological dimensions. When sitting with ayahuasca, you may expand your awareness to more subtle dimensions of your being, what Hindus may call the subtle or astral body. In the non-physical multidimensional space, you can encounter spiritual beings who sometimes want to offer healing gifts to us.

If this experience happens to you, approach it with curiosity and discernment. You can judge the intention of a spiritual being through the feelings you have in your body. You can also ask the being if it is there to help you and is in service to the highest will of spirit. Remember, while you are a multidimensional being sharing space with numberless other beings throughout the cosmos, you still do have the power to express your sovereignty through your boundaries. It may also be a comfort to know that when you are consuming ayahuasca with an experienced shaman, they have protected the space so you are safe.

In all cases, good preparation is the best policy. If you are participating in ceremony with an experienced shaman leader and with strong prayers for your guides and ayahuasca to protect you, you can most often trust whatever beings show up.

Ego Death

Ego death is a pretty big topic of conversation in the psychedelic world, as these medicines have a strong reputation for being able to push the mind (or the soul) over the edge, allowing it to seemingly detach from, well, you! This type of experience can be referred to as an ego death, ego dissolution, or ego loss. Are you scared? You shouldn't be.

If I am being honest, I was uncertain where to put this content. Is this a physical journey? It sometimes may appear to be rather physically punishing when one is going through it. Or, perhaps this is a visionary journey, since the experience is more or less happening internally. Regardless, an ego death is definitely deeply challenging, and most shamans believe it is the Everest of ayahuasca.

The ego is the human personality which is experienced as the self and is in contact with the external world through perception. Put simply, ego is the Latin word for "I." If you were to write "I love you" in Latin, you would write *"ego amo te"*. Therefore, what is an ego death? According to Wikipedia, ego death is a "complete loss of subjective self-identity" and I think this is a great place to start.[1] In simpler terms, the ego is everything we know and believe ourselves to be.

Imagine everything you think you are, every opinion and set of beliefs you have, your most basic thoughts and feelings, and the things that you believe define you as a person, but were never actually yours to begin with. Consider that, throughout your human development, you have been a receiver of information and experiences, and just like a piece of computer software, all of this input has become your operating system. All of these external teachings eventually came together, creating you - a complex personality with wants and needs, desires and fears, life goals and notions of failures, beliefs about the world, and so on.

Now imagine all of this being stripped away from you. How desperately would you cling to it? Would you feel comfortable being afloat in a sea of non-self?

There are people who believe the ego is a bad thing, and I am here to say it most certainly is not! The ego serves many purposes, but most importantly it is a part of your unconscious mind programmed to keep you alive. However, if the ego is not regulated, you may feel superior to others, turn yourself into a victim, or make faulty decisions. I recall during a ceremony, my ego slunk out of a corner and seemingly tried to intercept the medicine. I decided to thank it, and then told it to step aside while ayahuasca steered the ship!

Here are some telltale signs you are operating from an imbalanced ego:

- Victimhood; always an external force preventing achievement
- Heavily critical or judgmental of others
- Needing to be right at all costs
- Jealousy or resentment when other people succeed
- Refusal to receive needed help

(continued...)

- Refusal to learn when things go wrong and to learn different ways to grow
- Taking everything personally and responding with high emotion

When the ego is imbalanced, ayahuasca can step in, helping reorient the recipient and dissolve boundaries between themselves and the objective world. Feelings of unity will split free the ego from the shimmer of self, becoming a single boundless stream of you, God, the universe, and everyone and everything in it.

People who experience an ego death during ayahuasca sometimes describe it as extremely disorienting and terrifying. They report feeling like they were actually dying and entering an entirely new world, leaving behind everything they knew and loved. They believed in that moment, it was the end of their lives. Because most societies have taught us to fear death, it carries a tremendous amount of darkness. We do not even want to think about death, let alone go through it, perhaps equating it with an eternity of nothingness. However, an ego death will show you that this is not the case. The continuation of awareness remains, even beyond our identity and everything we hold dear. Realizing the immortality of consciousness (despite the fact our bodies are temporary) can be paradigm-shifting and enlightening. People often leave these experiences no longer afraid of death and with a curiosity about the beautiful cycle of life.

Ego death, when the natural boundaries between you and the objective world have been obliterated and you feel at one with everything, can also be quite an ecstatic experience. What remains is an incredible feeling of deep love and connection.

Regardless of how it goes down, if you find yourself in an ego death situation, the best thing you can do is know that you are safe, surrender to the experience and let yourself exist in the moment. Feel grateful for the exposure to the truth and soak up the feelings of unity and connectedness so many of us deeply and unconsciously desire.

Visionary Journey

The visionary journey is important in deep shamanic work, especially with ayahuasca. Ayahuasca is most often described as a Goddess spirit who prefers to use imagery to communicate rather than symbolic left-brain languages. As indigenous shamans have long known and as current Western science is now understanding, the deep visual archetypes we see in our minds during shamanic work are highly meaningful and transformative.

In 1997, Benny Shanon, Professor of Psychology and researcher of ayahuasca, found that ayahuasca participants consistently saw similar visual themes such as serpents, felines, palaces, angels, forests, flowers, and ancient civilizations.[2] On the whole, ayahuasca visions often have a distinctly Amazonian feel to them, which makes sense considering that is the home source of the plant medicine. The Amazon rainforest is the most densely bio-diverse region of the world. The spirit of Gaia, our dear Mother Earth, is powerfully present there.

Oftentimes, the visual journey is more specific to your personal life circumstances. For instance, if you are feeling trapped in life, you may see yourself in a cage. If your feminine spirit of creativity and love has been repressed, maybe you will see a princess in a prison tower. The visionary journey on ayahuasca (or otherwise accessed, such as through meditation, drumming, or other master plants) often invokes ageless human archetypes, such as what we find in fairy and folk tales passed on over centuries or millennia.

As you journey deeper into your body, allowing the pains to be felt and released, while surrendering deeper into yourself, the visual experience will change. You may like to mentally take note of what you are seeing throughout. Your journey is your time to receive the messages you need for your current moment of growth. The next morning, mentally review the key themes just as you may recollect a dream from the night before. This is a good time to write a few notes or even draw a picture of what you saw. It is not at all uncommon for people to see their future lives unfolding in an ayahuasca journey.

As with the rest of your journey, the best thing to do with the visual journey is to just observe without attachment or aversion. If you see vivid bright fractal grids, that is totally normal. That is what ayahuasca wants you to see because that is what is useful for you. If you see nothing, that is fine too, as you did not need to see anything to receive the benefits of the medicine. You do not need to wish for more interesting visuals, nor should you be disturbed by what you are seeing. You are always safe and it is just a momentary experience that will soon shift and change into another experience.

Sacred Geometry

What an interesting phenomenon sacred geometry is! Close your eyes, and you may be launched into a world of patterns, symbols and structures sometimes related to nature, space, time, and form. If you are fortunate enough to experience sacred geometry, consider yourself lucky; seeing these incredible patterns of existence can be a profound and life-changing experience.

Sacred geometry visions are typically found with eyes closed. These visions can shift into kaleidoscope or recognizable shapes or images that are often vibrant, fast moving, and profoundly real. You may even be able to leverage these shapes like portals that open to other beings or into alternate dimensions. On the flip side, sacred geometry can be confusing or may not even seem logical or relevant. At times, these visions can feel wholly arresting in their intensity, leaving you feeling agitated or confused.

There are times when ayahuasca is relentless with Her presentation of imagery, and the best you can do is hold on for dear life. Perhaps this is Her opportunity to shake the snow-globe of our minds, so to speak, so we can purge and release deep rooted traumas and blockages. Unfortunately we can only use our brains to ponder what the Spirit is doing, as this ancient wisdom far exceeds anyone's ability to comprehend or describe.

Understanding sacred geometry is to be aware that all of nature is geometric. While these images can trigger a memory, a sensation in your body, or perhaps even a lesson, it is often an opportunity to not only understand how they correlate to our own lives, but also how there is a deep interconnection between us and everything in the Universe and beyond. Engaging with sacred geometry allows an exploration of your spirit, allowing for a deeper connection with life itself.

Consult (Consulta)

Some people experience a consultation, or consult with ayahuasca during their journeys, and it cannot be a more mind-blowing experience.

A consult can unfold in several ways. You may hear Her voice, almost as if someone is talking next to you, except it is not an external sound, rather an inner listening. Her voice is clear as a bell, is definitely permeating, and is not derived from your own thoughts. It is a dialog that you are very much not in control of and the words feel incredibly accurate. Alternatively, She may provide a consult through the presentation of specific imagery or story lines. Almost like watching a movie, She will show you aspects of your life and past experiences you would not ordinarily want to contemplate.

Another type of consult is what I can only refer to as a download. To me, it feels like trying to fill a paper cup (your brain) at Niagara Falls (ayahuasca). There are times She shares so much information that it becomes a series of major epiphanies one after the other. Like, Bam! This is why my kid is acting like a jerk. Bam! This is why I am blocking love. Bam! And bam! And bam! It sometimes gets so intense that I will jump up in ceremony and start writing the details in my journal. Granted, it is dark. And I am on the medicine. My scribble rarely amounts to anything coherent but I try.

I often envision Neo getting plugged into the Matrix for the first time when Morpheus says "This will feel a little weird." Now granted, you are not going to get a head jack at the base of your skull but drinking ayahuasca is most definitely the Red Pill. The information you receive during ceremony, in my humble opinion, is the result of ayahuasca allowing for optimal expanded consciousness, granting us access to the unlimited knowledge-base of the Universe.

Ayahuasca is the wisest Grandmother. She may often simply provide you with subtle clues to your question rather than an overt answer. Do your best to keep a clear and open mind and listen carefully. Be receptive to hear, see, and feel the messages She sends. Subtlety is key with ayahuasca, so be patient, be still, and listen. From the moment the medicine touches your lips, you are in communication with Her (and some say even before that). You may find hours, days, or weeks later that She answered your question without you even realizing it.

Her consults come out of nowhere, and it is a feeling of being hit with information. If it is a true consult, you will be absolutely certain. A consult is not a function of your own mind presenting desirable information or filling in the gaps of what we believe is true. There are often times when our minds may be running the script. Over time you will develop discernment about what is what. Is it your ego-mind, your higher Self, ayahuasca, or even another spirit speaking to you?

Ayahuasca never speaks in a panicked voice, nor one that inflates your ego into grandiosity. She is not going to tell you that you are the shaman-god-king of a distant nebula, incarnated on Earth to start a cult. Likewise, please do not think that after one or a handful of ceremonies with ayahuasca that there is any chance whatsoever that you have been given permission by Her to serve the medicine in your own circles. If you are chosen by Her to serve the medicine, you have years of intense training and many dietas ahead of you.

You can and should speak (silently, in your head) to ayahuasca during your journey. Do so with reverence: *"Dear Mother, I am here to heal. Tell me what I need to know. <Insert question here>. I am here in service to life and offer gratitude to you."* With gratitude, focus, and determination, you may experience a fruitful communication with ayahuasca.

Absolutely Nothing Journey

That is correct, absolutely nothing. It is pretty hard to believe, but some people have drunk copious amounts of ayahuasca and felt absolutely nothing. No visions. No purges. Nothing. No effect whatsoever.

I can imagine how absolutely disappointing and frustrating this would be. Preparing for weeks on end, dropping a chunk of your savings, taking time out of your busy schedule, often flying out of the country, feeling nervous in anticipation, only to drink the medicine and fall asleep on your mat. To top it off, the ceremony ends and everyone is raving about rainbows and butterflies, riding unicorns, and talking directly to God! But journey envy aside, there is hope! Do not despair if this happens to you; Ayahuasca will be working with you behind the scenes even if you do not realize it (and if you work with Her, She will be even more present).

Here are several reasons a journey can result in an absolutely nothing journey:

- Not adhering to the dieta in the weeks preceding a ceremony can affect your receptivity to the medicine. The most common culprits include recreational drugs, alcohol, and caffeine. Substances that are contraindicated can not only cause an absolutely nothing journey, but in some cases be dangerous. Following the dieta is essential to creating the best experience possible.

- People who are new to ayahuasca have a higher rate of having an absolutely nothing journey, as their serotonin type-2 receptors are less sensitive to DMT. It is an interesting fact that the more ayahuasca one consumes, the less is needed to feel the effects of the medicine.

- The ayahuasca brew itself may also be the cause. Younger plants have less DMT and some preparations have lower concentrations of the plant. If this is the case, following ceremony you will come to learn that other participants also did not have a very deep experience.

(continued…)

- Most people are unaware they are doing this, but they come to the ceremony fearful and as a result, they resist the ayahuasca. This affects the intensity of the medicine and how deep one goes. You cannot surrender to Her and control Her at the same time.

- Another reason you did not have an experience is because ayahuasca did not want you to have an intense (or even noticeable!) journey during ceremony. Her reasons are Her own. She will likely communicate with you in the days and weeks following ceremony.

Some might be tempted to drink more medicine, beyond what is healthy or recommended. I do not recommend this approach. Rather, it is healthier and safer to give your body a chance to adjust to the medicine. Over time you will have an experience that is discernible.

I might also add, often the medicine provides you with an experience after ceremony. Like way after. My own son, when starting with the medicine, had three back-to-back absolutely nothing experiences. He and I were quite disappointed (because we had expectations - shame on me) and in that moment, he decided he was not going to pursue a relationship with Her in the future. One month later, he spontaneously received downloads of information from Her and decided to sit again. His fourth ceremony was incredibly fruitful and he is back on the ayahuasca track and in alignment with Her on the plant medicine path. His experience is not uncommon as most people continue to dialogue with Her long after ceremony, whether through wakeful serendipitous occurrences that feel divinely inspired or in dream states.

If you experience an absolutely nothing ceremony, try meditating in the days and weeks after your ceremony and focus on continuing a dialog with Her. Communicate in ways that feel good for you, such as by writing or singing to Her. If you have sat with ayahuasca, She is now within your field and available for consultation and healing. Often it is our own receptivity that is needed to hear the messages, so do make a practice of listening.

What You will Feel Conclusion

So, what will you feel during your ayahuasca journey? Who knows! That is completely up to your spirit and the medicine. As you go into your ceremony, just be curious and open to the wonderment of it all. If you are fortunate to commune with ayahuasca, you are indeed very blessed. So, relax. Breathe. Observe. Feel. Be thankful. Witness what is happening and go with the flow.

Ayahuasca is very much a closed eye experience and for the first time, you will be seeing with eyes wide shut. If you are not fond of what you are experiencing, opening your eyes will likely end those visions and the conversation, and sadly the opportunity that was presented to you. When I am communing with the divine, I open my eyes only when the shaman calls for a second cup and when ceremony has concluded.

Your experience with ayahuasca, whether it is predominately physical or visual, can largely be influenced by how you show up to ceremony. There is so much more for you to experience. She will never cease to amaze you, and indeed, the spiritual journey never ends. You are not a passive participant in this process. Your breath, your willingness to be present and feel everything happening, and your agreement to "move with the medicine" will allow you to have the fullest experience possible.

As I mentioned several times, you may receive so much information during an ayahuasca journey. While taking notes during ceremony may not be possible, I highly encourage journaling immediately following or the morning after ceremony. Every hour that you wait, you have the potential to lose the details of what you learned and experienced. Even the finer details of the experience need to be journaled, because you may find they are the key to bigger learnings in the future. There are several blank pages available at the back of this book to start your personal journaling.

Release control. Release expectations. The amount of information the spirit of ayahuasca can offer you is limitless. Whatever happens, accept it is for your highest good. And don't forget to say thank you!

Story Time

In February 2022, I received some bad news from my doctor. Disease. Rather than getting into specifically what that disease was, I can simply tell you that it was scary and I did not want to deal with it. Rather than taking the doctor's treatment plan and next steps, I put a pin in the situation and decided to drink more medicine. I do not recommend this for everyone, but it was a decision that felt right to me at the time.

During a particularly intense ayahuasca yagé ceremony while

feeling the effects of the medicine incredibly strong, I informed the shaman of this disease. (I am intentionally not calling it "my disease", as it was never mine to begin with.) This was the first time I ever spoke of it, since I told not one single soul. Even uttering the words made me feel awful.

The shaman performed a tobacco healing by blowing smoke over the area that was affected. Following the tobacco healing, he performed an incredibly intense limpia. Then he put his hand on my head, and said a prayer. Now, I do not know exactly what he was saying, as the chants are not in English. However, I did feel something very powerful permeate my brain, body, and soul in that moment. I was unclear what had just happened, but I knew something happened and it felt surreal. When the healing was over, I army crawled back to my space in the maloca (I did mention I was heavily under the influence of ayahuasca, right?) and flopped onto my bed. Off I went…

The next six hours were a blur and I was in and out of what felt like an alternate dimension. I kept trying to ground myself back on Planet Earth, to no avail. I thought I was slipping into psychosis and I was absolutely terrified. As with every single ceremony before, I eventually became grounded, and then sobered.

The morning following ceremony, I sat with the shaman and explained my experience as best I could. I asked him what he did when he put his hand on my head and his reply shook me to my core.

He asked God to send me back to the beginning of creation, where time and space do not exist. The shaman explained that I could not obtain the highest level of physical healing in this third dimension and that is where I needed to be.

To date, that was the most powerful, confusing, overwhelming, beautiful experience of my life and those are just a partial list of adjectives I can use to describe it. In the days and weeks following the single most intense metaphysical experience of my life, I tried to sit with it and grab as many details as possible to help give it shape, but my attempts were futile. The experience was completely ineffable in every aspect of the word and I have given up trying to understand it. I surrendered to complete and utter reverence and gratitude to Her and to the shaman that facilitated Her wishes.

In August 2022, I visited a new specialist in the field of this particular disease. And you want to hear something amazing? I had no disease. Nothing. My body is free from whatever darkness was in my body.

My dear Mitra Politi, you are a powerful knowledgeable experienced shaman, and I am eternally grateful for your wisdom, gentle healing, and blessing. I am forever in awe of our beautiful Grandmother and your ability to facilitate healing. Thank you!

Chapter 9
What Is a Purge & Why It Is Necessary

See it, and watch it change!

I recall a particularly tough journey where I purged in more than one way simultaneously for a considerable amount of time. On this particular night, the purging just would not end. While this is not very common, it does happen for some from time to time. In my experience, it is usually a prelude to an amazing finale.

What a cantankerous baby I can be! I am the master at making things a thousand times more miserable than they need to be, feeding into and enhancing every painful experience to the nth degree. Following what was the last of my purge that night, I collapsed on my mat, weak but incredibly grateful the purging seemed to be over. I sat in contemplation about what a purge actually is and why it is such an integral part of the process. That is when She spoke to me:

"How can I add to a cup that is already full?"

What Westerners would consider a side-effect is actually central to the therapeutic purpose of working with ayahuasca. The purge is designed to rid our bodies of trauma, limiting beliefs, and anything else that does not serve us. She is making room for new and healthy information and providing an opportunity for healing. She is not dissuaded by the mere moments of discomfort we may endure. The wonderful gift She provides is not only the opportunity to eliminate what does not serve us, but the strength to get through it. When you understand why we purge, you can understand and appreciate what an unbelievable blessing purging actually is.

In many shamanic cultures and practices there is no separation between the body and the mind, which also means there is no separation between self and nature--the body is after all a natural organism. In these cultures, creating balance is central to overall health and wellness. This integrative-naturalistic ideology is becoming more widespread in mainstream health, no doubt shaping a better understanding of where disease comes from. So, although purging is often a process that involves the physical body, it is very much ayahuasca's way to expel what causes imbalance in the mind as well as in order to restore us to health and vitality.

Consider this metaphor: Imagine you have been living in the same house for decades. You never bothered to change the furniture, even though it is dated, stained, and broken. The house is messy and dusty because you lack the energy to clean it. In almost every room, something needs repair. Your home exudes an extraordinarily low energy that is hard to ignore. Does the image of this house make you want to run away from it? Yeah, me too.

Much to your delight (or dismay), an angel stops by. They begin the process of discarding the old furniture, cleaning up the mess, fixing the things that need repair, and raising the energy. During this process, you may be tempted to say, "Oh wait, I want to keep that!" or "Don't throw that away, that has sentimental value." But the angel knows you are desperate to hold on to things that no longer serve you. They simply wave their hand and proceed. The angel decorates your home beautifully. New clean furniture. Everything is shining! You walk around and feel the improved energy and your home now brings a sense of joy and wonder.

The house is you. Ayahuasca is the angel.

When ayahuasca comes up in conversation, most people are intent on talking about purging. While this is certainly one component of the medicine, I find it short-sighted and unfortunate that people will not partake in a ceremony because of this potential. Purging can take many forms, and it may not happen at all.

Most people will agree, the medicine is designed to heal our bodies, rid us of trauma and disease, help us unearth and understand unhealthy patterns and conditioning, and bring a host of other benefits as well. Yet, with all this wonderful potential, many are unwilling to experience temporary discomfort due to physical purging. Talk about a missed opportunity!

While ayahuasca can be physically and mentally challenging at times, here is another way to think about the purge. If you get a virus, your body does whatever is necessary to get rid of it. You vomit, have diarrhea, sweat, shake, etc. If your body does not do the work to rid itself of the virus, it will overtake your organs and you will die. It is that simple.

Now imagine that virus is trauma. Or shame. Or anger. Or preconceived ideas about who you are as a person which dim your light or create discontent. Ayahuasca works to rid your body of this. She does not care that you will be uncomfortable for an hour or so. She knows these things will make you sick. Feel some discomfort now on your terms by consuming ayahuasca, or suffer later when being treated for illness.

So, what might be purged? Here are my conclusions from personal experiences:

- The buildup of toxins, from processed foods, environmental pollutions, pharmaceuticals, drugs, electromagnetic radiation.
- Trauma stored in your body due to victimhood, hurt, and disappointment.
- Emotions, reactions, or other true feelings that were suppressed because of embarrassment, wanting to look strong, or wanting to be considered normal and be loved.
- Every time you acted inauthentically because of how you were conditioned to believe and shamed for wanting to do otherwise.
- Anger, resentment, guilt, shame, and any other feeling that was ignored, minimized, or ridiculed instead of honored and released.
- Feeling unworthy, ugly, stupid, invisible, or not respected.
- Trauma, pain, and dysfunction from past lives and ancestors.

Most of us come to the medicine with decades of this shit. While we can identify some of our baggage easily, we all have unexplored rooms, hidden closets, and locked safes in the mansion of the unconsciousness, which can be identified and purged during ceremony. If you do not deal with it in one way or another, it has the potential at best to diminish your quality of life.

Here's where my tough mothering will show itself. So, you are uncomfortable for a moment. So what! Did you ever contemplate how much of your strength came from discomfort? Have you considered there is benefit to purposeful discomfort and that embracing it can play an important role in your personal growth? When we face our pain head on and have a careful plan to work with it, we can transform and move past it. While burying, hiding, or ignoring the trauma that lives in your body is most certainly possible (and the majority of our human population does this constantly), it is impossible to transform it without examining it so you can understand and own it. Embracing it all, both joy and pain, can be equally helpful along your spiritual path. You are strong, no matter what you tell yourself.

When you sit with ayahuasca, you bring a great light of presence into the chambers of your soul that you had otherwise abandoned or neglected to explore or inhabit in your life. She helps you clean house of any exploitative energies, views, beliefs, ideas, or values that are not aligned with your highest truth and wellbeing.

You can and should continue the purging process of ayahuasca after your nights of drinking the medicine. Following the ceremony and after returning to the center of your new life, you may be tasked with purging addictions, people, roles, habits, and any other context that reinforces your limitations and false self.

In ceremony, there are many types of purging, and not everyone will experience all or sometimes any of them. *"See it, and watch it change"* is a mantra I have become accustomed to internally chanting during ceremony. It means there is absolutely no need to get attached to anything you are experiencing in ceremony because every sensation, visualization, and experience is incredibly impermanent. The medicine will always react differently depending on what the person needs and how they are handling their process.

As Grandmother Ayahuasca whispered to me once during ceremony, *"Suffering is a choice"*. We can get attached to and feed into every sensation during a purge and make the experience miserable. Or, we can thank Her for each and every opportunity to heal and learn and grow. It is up to you. Suffering is a choice in ceremony, and well, in life too!

Vomit Purge

This is the most common and frequently spoken of type of purge. While it is a highly common type of purge experience, accounting for 70% of participants, here are some tips on how to mitigate or lessen a vomit purge.

- Ensure you are adhering to a good six to eight hour fast before ceremony so your body is not inundated with food. This will help the medicine digest more quickly.

- Clear juice is acceptable up until four hours before ceremony. Water is acceptable up until one hour before ceremony.

- Following the consumption of the medicine, sit upright with spine erect for at least 30 minutes. Gravity and alignment will help move the medicine through your body.

- If you become tired after you drink, lay down slowly. The earlier stages of consuming the medicine are not the time to jostle your body around, dance, or go for a walk.

- Lay on your left side. The stomach's natural position is on the left side where the medicine can digest more effectively.

- Do not drink water during the actual ceremony. Water will ferment the medicine and increase your nausea.

- Breathe. Sometimes our minds can get carried away and make us feel nauseous without reason. Take deep slow breaths in through the nose and out through the mouth.

There is a difference between a vomit purge and simply throwing up. If you find yourself head first in your bucket within ten to fifteen minutes of consuming the medicine, you are likely not having a purge. There are a handful of people who have a very strong reaction to the taste of the medicine and if you fall into this category, consuming a small mint immediately following each cup may help. Mint is an antispasmodic so it can mitigate nausea and help with digestion. Another trick I have learned along the way is consuming a few saltine crackers before drinking ayahuasca. Saltine crackers can help absorb gastric acid and may allay an immediate reaction to the medicine. Don't overdo it though as food can interfere with the absorption of the medicine.

Never leave your bucket behind. If you need to go to the bathroom, go for a walk, or drink more medicine, always bring your bucket. Vomit purges can come on quickly, so you always want your bucket within arm's reach. Bring your bucket! Bring your bucket! Bring your bucket!

If you do vomit purge, some recommend trying to do so quietly and meditatively. This isn't always possible, but the process of eliminating trauma is sacred and remaining calm and centered can make you more comfortable. Trust your body and trust the medicine. The process underway is far more ancient and intelligent than your conditioned mind. The more relaxed you can be, the easier it will be. You also want to be mindful of other participants in the room.

There can be times when you feel very nauseous for an extended period of time, but the purge doesn't happen. Sometimes ayahuasca needs time to delve into the nooks and crannies of your being, uprooting energies and deep-seated traumas. She is navigating decades of your existence, working, learning, and navigating a complex system, so be patient with this process. It can take several ceremonies for the channels in your body to open into fuller release. Please know, as unpleasant as you may feel, you absolutely cannot and should not force a vomit purge. It is imperative that you relax and breathe into this sensation. The more you relax, the more ayahuasca is able to move and work through you.

When nausea is prolonged or a vomit purge feels stuck, it sometimes helps to shift your position and gently move around. If you are curled up in the fetal position, open your body so stuck energy can shift. Roll over and lay on the other side of your body. Some find laying on their belly helps. Stretch! And as dreadful as this may sound in that moment, drinking more ayahuasca can shift this sensation or trigger a purge. Finally, you will learn about sacred snuff in Chapter 10, which can help alleviate nauseas or bring on a purge.

If you are going to vomit purge, it is best to allow gravity to help the process. Do not attempt to purge sitting up, or lying down. Ideally, you will be on all fours, with the bucket under your shoulders.

Purging Pro-Tip: Now, this may sound totally bonkers, but keep an open mind for just a moment. Following a vomit purge, look at the purge and ask, "What are you?" If you are of the opinion that a purge is designed to rid our bodies of trauma, limiting beliefs, and anything that does not serve us, perhaps you want to know what it was that you just got rid of. People have reported seeing faces or objects in their purge buckets that mean something significant to them. It can be described as the physical manifestation of emotions that were previously trapped inside the body.

Diarrhea / Bottom Purge

Diarrhea is also a common type of purge. It can happen once or throughout the night. Diarrhea can also happen the following day or days after consuming the medicine.

I know it is a sensitive topic but it is time for some finer details on the bottom purge. It is pretty clear that the number one fear prior to an ayahuasca ceremony is soiling oneself. I cannot say that it has not concerned me too, nor would I be okay with this happening. However, it is rare. Like, really rare. I have sat with thousands of people during ceremony and only a handful of people had an issue.

Keep in mind that during an ayahuasca ceremony, you usually have the ability to get up, walk, talk, ask for help, etc. So, if you have to go, go. If you are working with professionals, there will be facilitators who will walk you to the bathroom if you do not feel stable or capable enough to do it yourself. And if there is an issue, they will be incredibly helpful and discreet.

Here are some tips:

- Never trust an ayahuasca fart! No need to elaborate on this one. When in doubt, go to the bathroom.

- If you are at a facility that offers colonics, take advantage of that service before ceremony.

- Some participants really never get over the fear of soiling themselves, so I recommend wearing an adult diaper in ceremony. Whatever makes you more comfortable will ultimately benefit your ceremony. While I do not know too many who have not made it to the bathroom in time, this does give some people a sense of security.

Yawning

Believe it or not, yawning is a type of purge, but we are not talking about any ordinary yawn. These are overly exaggerated, mile-long yawns where your jaw feels like it is going to unhinge, your mouth feels a foot wide, and it is often accompanied with sound. Ordinary yawns have a relaxing effect on the nervous system; Ayahuasca yawns feel like ancient stress releasing.

Shaking / Trembling / Shivering

Some may experience mild twitching or trembling. Others may experience excessive trembling throughout their whole body, which can last hours.

Shaking is a great way for energy to move and purge itself from the body. Imagine energy or emotions stuck in your cellular memory, and the only way to release them is to shake them loose. Have you ever seen an animal being chased by a predator? Oftentimes, after escaping, they will shake free the fear and adrenaline.

If the medicine has settled and you are feeling steady on your feet, dancing can be very cathartic and healing. Alternatively, a nice big stretch and deep breathing can help release that energy as well.

Sweating

I don't mean a few drops on your forehead— I mean sweating profusely! This is an easy type of purge, as it feels natural and is pain free. To sweat is a sacred act and used to heal and purify. For example, sweat lodges are common purification practices in

North and Central America for cleansing and healing purposes. We have all experienced sweating with a fever. It is a great way for the body to regulate body temperature, release stress, and improve skin clarity, organ function, and circulation. Sweating also reduces stress hormones and helps rebalance our adrenal hormones.

Feeling Intensely Hot or Cold

The feeling of being intensely hot or cold can come in waves. One minute you are freezing and the next minute you are blazing hot. Dress in layers and have your blanket ready for sudden shifts in these temperature sensations.

Spontaneous Movements

Spontaneous movements are studied in many spiritual practices, and in yoga are known as kriyas. During the ceremony, the unconscious mind opens up and allows suppressed emotions to come to the surface. This can result in random, sometimes jerky movements. These are simply outward expressions of the movement of our inner energy. Do not be embarrassed, as this is just another form of energetic release. Good thing it is dark in the maloca!

Laughing

Gangaji said, "If you're laughing, you're healing." And really, what is more awesome than big-belly laughter? Some people break out into uncontrollable laughter while on the medicine. What usually follows is a contagion that touches every person in the room until the echoes of happiness boomerang off the walls. Laughter is my favorite form of purging.

Sighing, Moaning

Audible sighs and non-sexual moaning are both pretty common during ceremony. These sounds are known to relieve stress, negative emotions, panic, and pain, and encourage relaxation.

Spontaneous Vocalizations / Sleep Talking

There can be a lot of chatter during a ceremony from participants who are either asleep, awake and aware, or entranced. Some participants can have full, inner-dialogue conversations and are clearly reliving earlier life experiences, resolving conflicts and navigating psychic complexes that were never worked out. You may even hear screaming and obscenities along the way. Do not be alarmed, as these are all purges and ways to release energy.

Usually a handful of people fall into a deep sleep during ceremony, which has always made me a little jealous. Why do they get to slumber as I walk through the valley of the shadow of death? Everyone has different work to do and the medicine may just want them to be unconscious while She does it. Be prepared for the snorer.

Crying

I am not talking about a few tears. I am talking ugly crying, face distorted, nose running, face soaked, audible. But man, does it feel amazing! This is the type of purge that can release so much suppressed emotion and is thus quintessential in healing. These tears may not only be repressed emotions, but can represent cathartic love in the forgiveness of yourself or others or extreme gratitude for the medicine or the millions of other things to be grateful for. You may not even know why you are crying, and that is okay. Just let it all out; you may become aware of the reasons later.

Alternatively, many experience tears without actually feeling sad. You may wake with tears collected on your face.

Anxiety / Panic Attacks

While anxiety during ceremony may or may not be a purge, I want to address this potential response so you can be prepared. A panic attack is a feeling of sudden and intense anxiety. Symptoms of a panic attack include increased heart rate, breathlessness, hyperventilation, feeling dizzy or disoriented, and a dry mouth.

Fear not! Although the symptoms of a panic attack can make you feel like you are in mortal danger, you are safe and it will pass. Most panic attacks last anywhere from five minutes to half an hour.

Some techniques to help:

- Breath is the life force. Practicing deep breathing techniques can mitigate a panic attack and allow for the medicine to work more efficiently. Reacquaint yourself with several practices outlined in Chapter 5. Inhale through the nose for a very slow count of ten, and exhale from your mouth for a slow count of fifteen. See your belly rise on the inhale and fall on the exhale. Do this several times.

- Muscle tension is a big culprit in making your body feel like it is in danger. While practicing your slow breathing techniques, progressive muscle relaxation aims to release tension in one group of muscles at a time to relax the whole body. Scan your body and release tension.

- I am fairly obsessed with the Mammalian or Ice Diving Technique as it is truly the greatest trick in the book. We possess a dive reflex, which is activated when we put cold water on our faces or submerge ourselves in cold water. The reflex activates the parasympathetic nervous system, thus slowing the heart rate. If you are able, make your way to the restroom and splash cold water onto your face. Do this several times until you feel calmer.

- Smile. By smiling, you are telling the nervous system that you are safe and everything is okay. It signals to your brain to release dopamine, endorphins and serotonin which are associated with lowering your anxiety and increasing feelings of happiness.

- Soothing mental talk or mantras may help as well. Try repeating in your mind, "I am safe. It is okay to relax and let go." Speak to yourself in a slow and calm manner. Sometimes, you need to just climb into the cockpit and steady the plane.

Transmutation Purge

I am writing this immediately following ceremony, one in which Grandmother Ayahuasca was very generous with information. What I have recently come to learn by sitting with the medicine is that physical purging is not always a requirement.

To transmute by definition is to change something completely, especially into something different and better. Alchemy is the practice of transmuting base metals to gold or transforming things from one form to another as if by magic. Spiritual alchemy is the transmuting of lower nature or negative situations or experiences to those of a higher nature.

What this means is that as these energies are brought to the surface, you are presented with a choice: purge them in any of the ways listed above, or transmute the energy and release it.

When energy emerges that requires release it can be intense, causing discomfort, pain, confusion, and anxiety. Transmuting a purge requires awareness and steadfastness. The first step is to simply notice. Not in a frantic, this-has-to-change, how-do-I-escape this noticing but with an understanding and acknowledgement that something that no longer serves you is coming up and you have an opportunity to release it. Don't run. Be brave and face it head on. If you are feeling anxious, go back to your breathing exercises and do a body scan to release areas of tension.

In tandem with noticing, surrender and trust the medicine to support the process of transmuting energy that no longer serves you. I know from firsthand experience, the state of surrender and trust is incredibly challenging as it seems our default mode is to resist. While your brain and body may be on high alert, know that surrender and trust in Her will help get you through this.

Transmuting a purge also requires curiosity and investigation. While the exploration of pain is not something we are encouraged to do, getting up close and having dialog with this energy can help you discover its root, and show you how to heal it. So, have a chat with this energy and ask questions. Notice where the pain is showing up in your body. Is there an unhealed part of you that is being revealed? What could be the origins of this stuck energy? As you explore it, accept yourself and any feelings that may be coming up with loving kindness. This is hard work and you are doing the best you can!

As you stay with this process, gratitude goes a long way. Ceaselessly thanking the medicine for allowing healing to happen will shift the experience into a positive one. It is hard to be thankful when you are uncomfortable, but having a healthy perspective that this is for your betterment can make all the difference.

Purge Conclusion

With all these types of purging going on simultaneously, the maloca can sound pretty funny. Laughing, crying, vomiting, yawning, moaning and groaning all at once in a dark maloca may make it seem like you are in the bowels of hell. You are not. Rather, you are experiencing the most amazing opportunity you will ever be in!

Try not to judge or get sucked into others' experience. Whatever you are hearing is their experience, not yours. If you find yourself getting irritated, you may want to ask yourself where else do you feel irritated in life and how has it affected you? What tools can you use in ceremony to refocus your attention and feel more at peace and can you take these tools with you in daily life?

Purging is a completely natural, safe, and yes, good and healthy part of the ayahuasca experience. Purging is not a "side effect" on your way to receiving DMT visions in the third eye. Rather, it reflects the core purpose of ayahuasca: cleaning our bodies and minds of garbage so that we may live with freedom and love. Trust is the most important factor for purging, and knowing that you are in the hands of an ancient healing master. Surrender and relax into the experience.

With this chapter's overview of the many possible purges, I hope you feel safe and ready to navigate whatever comes up on your ayahuasca journey.

Chapter 10
Plant Medicines that Support Ayahuasca

The first time I attended an ayahuasca ceremony, I witnessed people ingesting all sorts of powders, potions, and cocktails in their mouth, nose, eyes, and through their skin. It appeared to be a real Smorgasbord of plant medicines. I have since come to learn there are many plant medicine allies used before, during, and after an ayahuasca ceremony as well as in your daily life.

While ayahuasca is complete and needs no help or improvement, there are certain plant medicines that augment and support your overall experience. Before, during, and after ceremony (or simply as a stand-alone practice), certain plant medicines can improve visions, quiet the mind, release negative sensations, ground you during a rough patch, and act as an emotional salve. The plant medicines I discuss here are often served to help support your ayahuasca journey.

Plant medicines such as sacred snuff, mapacho, ambil and mambé, cacao, sananga and lemongrass water each have a purpose and a place in your body. With understanding, you can leverage each plant medicine's power in ceremony, and in day-to-day life as well. Keep in mind, just as with ayahuasca, it is best to consume these plant medicines on an empty stomach. Having a full stomach may interfere with their absorption and increase your chances of nausea.

Before getting into the plant medicines that have a symbiotic relationship with ayahuasca, I want to share what is in complete dissidence with the medicine. Unfortunately, there is an emergence of retreat centers offering master plant medicines in tandem with ayahuasca. I believe this stems in part from the recent trend of "drug tourism" and is a way for facilities to lure in more participants. Many experienced shamans strongly discourage consuming master plant medicines in tandem with ayahuasca. Combining heavy hitters like psilocybin mushrooms, Bufo alvarius (5-MeO-DMT), peyote, San Pedro, cannabis, and other entheogens alongside ayahuasca is dangerous and contraindicated. Each of these beautiful plant medicines have their own way of communicating with you and deserve their own time in the sun so to speak.

Sacred Snuff (a.k.a. Rapé or Hapé)

There are many plant medicines in an ayahuasca ceremony but there is one that definitely takes center stage: sacred snuff. Sacred snuff is also known as rapé (pronounced "ra-peh"), hapé (pronounced "ha-peh"), or sacred tobacco; these terminologies are used interchangeably and are generally all appropriate. For purposes of this conversation, I will refer to this plant medicine as rapé.

This wondrous medicine has been used for sacred spiritual practices for thousands of years. It dates back to the time of the Incas and it is believed to be connected to the discovery of tobacco's psychotropic properties. Needless to say, it's kind of a big deal.

What is Rapé?

Rapé is a complex blend of pulverized Amazonian medicinal plants, trees, leaves, seeds, and other sacred ingredients. However, the true heart of most rapé blends is the Amazonian tobacco species known as nicotiana rustica (also known as mapacho; more details on mapacho as a stand-alone medicine start on page 225).

Don't confuse nicotiana rustica with nicotiana tabacum (common tobacco), the type of tobacco found in cigarettes.[1] Nicotiana rustica does not have the thousands of harmful chemicals found in common tobacco, but it is much stronger. It is said to contain up to twenty times the amount of nicotine found in common tobacco!

In addition to nicotiana rustica, rapé may include the following:[2]
- Ash, burned from the bark of local trees
- Non-tobacco plants such as: tonka bean, banana peels, cinnamon, clove buds, camphor laurel exudate, cassava, Peruvian cocoa
- Individual chemicals such as: coumarin, camphor, mint/menthol, eugenol
- Alkaline ashes (calcium carbonate)

Some rapé recipes include more powerful ingredients such as the leaves of the Banisteriopsis caapi tree (the ayahuasca vine), anadenanthera peregrina (also known as yopo, jopo, cohoba, parica or calcium tree), jurema, and coca.[3] When such a power-plant is added, the rapé can cause a very powerful psychotropic reaction.

The process of making rapé is sacred and labor intensive, and can often take days.[4] Tobacco leaves along with the other ingredients are air cured or heated over a low fire. Everything is then pulverized and finely sifted. What remains is a fine ground up powder that is light as air!

Rapé is completely legal in the United States and in most parts of the world. If you plan on purchasing rapé for personal use, have a conversation with the tribe who made the plant medicine, or at the very least the person sourcing it from the tribe. Keep your questions simple by asking how strong the medicine is, what the effects are for that particular blend, and what are the ingredients. Some rapé blends do not contain tobacco at all. While some recipes are kept secret, you should be informed what the main ingredients are and how they can affect you. Some e-retailers also have product reviews which can offer insights from other consumers.

From my experience, some rapé blends are mild and very tolerable, while others are very strong and can have a lasting effect. Just like in the preparation of ayahuasca or other herbal and plant medicines, the energies and intentions of the tribe, herbalist or shaman are also infused into the medicine. Be sure your rapé was made in the right relationship with the plants by people who have a pure intent.

These are reputable sources for rapé applicators and blends:

- Four Visions Market: https://fourvisionsmarket.com
- Sacred Flows: https://sacredflowstudios.com

The folks at the above markets are happy to share knowledge about rapé and their blends and answer any questions you may have.

How Rapé is Consumed

While rapé is typically used before, during, and/or after an ayahuasca ceremony, anyone can use and experience this medicine in the comfort of their own home as a tool for spiritual connection and healing. The recommended frequency and intention for using rapé vary by tribe. It can be used before breakfast, lunch or dinner by some, or simply when you want to connect to the plant medicine. Just keep in mind, when consuming rapé, give it the same reverence as you would ayahuasca or any other plant medicine.

Rapé is administered in the nose, but it is not snorted or inhaled. Rather, it is forcefully blown into the nose. Depending on how you are receiving the medicine, various tools can be used to administer rapé.

Rapé Self-Administration via a Kuripe

Single Nostril Kuripe

Double Nostril Kuripe

Rapé Administered via a Tepi
by a Shaman, or other qualified individual

Single Nostril Tepi

Double Nostril Tepi

When self-administering rapé, you have complete control as to which blend and how much you consume as well as how hard you blow it into your nose. When receiving rapé from a shaman, all bets are off. She/he will determine which blend to administer, along with how much and how forcefully she/he will blow. While there are some shamans that may provide a small window for dialogue, some suggest trusting that they intuitively know what to serve you. I have received rapé from shamans that took over an hour to integrate. While you have the right to request what you feel is best, this is still an act of surrender and not for the faint of heart. Receiving rapé from a facilitator is more of a middle ground. They may ask how much rapé you would like to receive, and how hard of a blow you prefer.

Prior to receiving rapé:

- It is important you are intentionally aligned when using rapé. Respecting the plant medicine, creating an intention, and clearing your mind are all priorities.

- Be especially observant if you are responding to a calling to consume rapé, or if you are reacting to a craving.

(continued...)

- As with any plant medicine, your set and setting are essential. (See Chapter 2 for more details on this.) Your mindset should be clear and conscientious. Your setting should be relatively quiet and sacred. This is not a medicine you want to consume in your car at a red light or in line at the DMV. Rapé deserves your undivided attention, so plan to carve out at least fifteen minutes to sit with the medicine after you have received it.

- Have everything you will need in front of you: tissues, water, a receptacle to spit into, and anything else necessary to be comfortable.

If it is your first time self-administering rapé, I suggest asking someone with experience for guidance. If you are not in ceremony, you can likely find someone to sit with virtually. At the very least, there are some great online videos that share different perspectives and means of receiving this medicine. My go-to video on YouTube was created by one of my first rapé teachers, Carlos Guzman, entitled *Introduction to Sacred Use of Rapé*.[5]

Pro tip: There is a muscle behind your nose that, when engaged, will stop the flow of air. You can feel it when you swallow or you may engage it when going underwater. When properly engaged, you will only be able to breathe out of your mouth. Before receiving rapé, engage that muscle and keep it engaged for two to four minutes following the medicine. This will stop the rapé from getting in your throat, causing you to choke and swallow the medicine. Practice engaging this muscle, so when you receive rapé, you will be saved from some discomfort. If you are receiving rapé from a shaman, engage it more intensely and do not forget to receive the medicine at the very top of an inhale. Shamans typically blow rapé much harder than you or a facilitator would. Ah, but it feels oh so good!

To self-administer rapé using a single nostril kuripe:

- Place a pea-sized amount of rapé in your palm.

If this is the first time you are using a specific blend, start with a smaller amount until you know its strength and how you will react to it.

- With your kuripe, flatten and smooth out the rapé in your palm to ensure there are no lumps.

(continued...)

- Scoop the rapé into the long pipe of your kuripe. When you are adding the medicine to the kuripe, do so towards your heart. You are connecting the medicine to your body.

- Once your kuripe is loaded up, put the long end of the pipe into your left nostril and the short end into your mouth. At the top of an inhale with your mouth, give your kuripe one big blow or a short sequence of quick, strong blows.

- Make sure your eyes are closed when you receive the medicine. If rapé gets in your eyes, it will burn. Also, do not breathe rapé in through your mouth, as it will cause you to choke and gag.

- Within one to two minutes, repeat on the right side.

It is imperative that both nostrils receive rapé to promote balance. Do not skip the other side, no matter what you are feeling or your reaction to the medicine. Both sides need to receive the same amount of rapé, each within a short period of one another.

To self-administer rapé using a double nostril kuripe, do your best to ensure both pipes are evenly filled with rapé and simply follow the same steps as outlined above.

Carlos Guzman's video provides some wonderful tips on how to set intentions and offer gratitude to the rapé prior to consuming. To summarize, before administering rapé, place the kuripe with the medicine in it on your third eye (in between your eyebrows) and set your intentions. Your intentions can be anything, but suggestions that work well with rapé include requesting healing, help with clarity, alignment with your true self, creating calmness, and opening of your true path. After you have set your intentions, hold the kuripe to your heart and offer gratitude. Maybe you will offer thanks to the people who worked tirelessly to make the medicine. Or perhaps you want to thank the tribal ancestors who passed along this wisdom for thousands of years for our benefit.

While under the effects of ayahuasca, you may have the opportunity to request rapé from the shaman or a facilitator and there are several reasons for doing so.

- If you are struggling for a prolonged period of time, rapé received at the right moment can really help in your process.

- Rapé can alleviate a thought loop, which is a chain of thoughts or emotions that repeats itself over and over.

(continued...)

- Rapé can ground you back in your body and your breath, relieving anxiety.

- If you are experiencing nausea for an extended period of time, rapé can bring on a purge that feels stuck.

Be advised, it may be challenging to self-administer rapé during ceremony. Ceremony space is often dark, and being under the effects of ayahuasca can make it unsafe to do so.

How Does Rapé Feel

There are hundreds, if not thousands of rapé blends, each with different ingredients and concentrations. Therefore, every blend will provide varied effects and for varied durations. I have my two favorites, Yawanawa and Nawa, which are both feminine and light, but sometimes I go for the heavy hitters and feel its effects for over an hour.

When rapé is blown into the nose, it reaches the olfactory region of the brain and enters the bloodstream. There are a few physical sensations that are immediate but are not very long-lasting including a burning sensation in the nose, watery eyes, a strong tingling sensation in the scalp and/or brain (generally on the side that received the rapé), and excessive salivation. Excessive spitting following receiving rapé is very common. Keep in mind, rapé can act as a purgative for many, so any type of purge can occur. Just relax! Close your eyes, breathe slowly, and focus on your intention as the effects of the rapé start to set in.

Shortly after receiving rapé, you may feel the following sensations that can last anywhere from ten minutes to an hour:

- Release of toxins, primarily through excessive saliva resulting in spitting, runny nose / mucus, nasal secretions, watery eyes, coughing
- Experience a purge, most commonly sweating
- Release physical tensions, resulting in relaxed, peaceful state
- Decreased mental chatter, calm mind
- Feeling more emotionally grounded, allowing clarity and reduced anxiety
- Improved focus; sharp mind, acute attention and awareness
- Answers or clarity of your intentions may be made known

The long-term physical, mental, and spiritual benefits of rapé may include:[6]

- Detoxes both body and mind and clears your energetic field
- Opens the third eye
- Decalcifies the pineal gland which naturally hardens and calcifies with age
- Clears and purifies sinuses of mucus and bacteria, thereby helping to combat colds and respiratory ailments
- Supports the digestive system, moves the bowels
- Strengthens the immune system
- Provides energetic protection when connected, providing strength, clarity, and focus

Every blend of rapé has different energies, qualities and outcomes due to the ingredients used, and the prayers they are infused with.

Rapé Risks and Considerations

In an effort to be thorough, I will share rapé's risks, potential adverse effects and health concerns so you can best decide if this medicine is something you wish to explore further.

A very thorough analysis and research paper, "Comprehensive chemical characterization of Rapé tobacco products: Nicotine, un-ionized nicotine, tobacco-specific N'-nitrosamines, polycyclic aromatic hydrocarbons, and flavor constituents," examined the contents of various Amazonian rapé blends, some with and some without tobacco.[7] The article is extensive, but in short, some of the blends had chemicals that were carcinogenic, and by-products of combustion. Some of the rapé studied had nicotine ranging from 6.32 to 47.6 milligram per gram of sample, which on the high end, is considered incredibly high. (The average cigarette has an average of 8 milligrams.) Some research suggests certain blends of rapé may even contain heavy metals. Always know who you are sourcing your medicine from.

In addition to the contents of various rapés being suspect, a great many people use the medicine and are addicted to it. It is imperative to be mindful when consuming rapé, and not to use it as a crutch. For so many reasons, I only consume rapé when in an ayahuasca ceremony, or on certain occasions in my home when I am contemplating something deeper that I need assistance with. At times, when I feel a calling for the medicine, I connect with it on an energetic level and do not consume it at all. Always be aware of when and why you are consuming it.

Mapacho

Mapacho is another wonderful master teacher plant, also known as nicotiana rustica, Aztec tobacco, or wild tobacco. It is a natural tobacco which has been a part of indigenous Amazonian rituals for centuries. According to Terence McKenna's book *Food of the Gods*, mapacho is a "much more potent, chemically complex, and potentially hallucinogenic" tobacco compared to nicotiana tabacum.

Ayahuasca is referred to as Grandmother and mapacho is Grandfather. It is a much stronger and purer version of tobacco, offering powerful healing, deep cleansing, grounding and clarity. The use of tobacco in the Amazon is unique as it is used in ceremony, rather than in mindless chain-smoking. Traditionally, a Tabaquero specializes in and serves mapacho.

How Mapacho is Consumed

Mapacho is incredibly versatile, offering recipients several ways to consume it. The following three techniques are some common ways of receiving the medicine:

- **Drinking:** Mapacho can be prepared and prayed over by the Tabaquero (tobacco shaman) as a strong brew, which is then drunk. Mapacho in tea form is typically consumed in its own ceremony and not alongside ayahuasca. Some retreats offer mapacho as a tea ceremony the morning of an ayahuasca ceremony because when consumed in large amounts, it induces vomiting. This purgative and cleansing experience prepares the body for the upcoming ayahuasca ceremony by clearing dense energies and ridding the body of lingering toxins. When we have an intentional relationship with tobacco and drink it, it carries both the shaman's and our intentions for healing.

- **Smoking:** In many shamanic traditions, smoke plays a vital role and is used as a way to clear, protect and carry intention. Mapacho smoke can be blown throughout and around the maloca prior to an ayahuasca ceremony to clear the energies and deter bad spirits from approaching. Shamans typically utilize mapacho during a healing ceremony by dragging a mapacho pipe or cigarette and blowing it on the recipient's head, hands or whole body, sending their healing energies and clearing power of the mapacho into the person's energetic field. You too can practice soplar, by dragging on a mapacho cigarette (do not inhale) and blowing it on your body. Just by holding the smoke in your mouth, you can deepen your relationship with mapacho, talking with the spirit of this medicine and receiving His knowledge and blessings.

- **Liquid Tobacco:** Liquid mapacho is made by soaking the leaves in water until the water itself becomes dense and has a dark tint. During this process, the water absorbs all the properties of the mapacho, especially the concentration of nicotiana rustica which is water soluble. The liquid is then poured into each nostril with a dropper or a small spoon, or the shaman will pour it into your hands and ask you to inhale it through your nose. The initial sensation can be quite uncomfortable. Some experience nausea, dizziness, or hiccups, which is actually a good sign that the medicine has begun to work. As it removes layers of blocked energies, recipients may notice a clearer and more open mind, and an increase in overall energy and strength. Generally, this ceremony includes at least three rounds of application, as this corresponds to the three doors of the three main healing channels – love, medicine and protection. After that, the recipient can choose to have more, which frequently happens. The ritual of inhaling liquid mapacho, or "repocati rao," has been passed down from generation to generation in the Shipibo culture.

How Does Mapacho Feel

As you can see, there are several ways to receive and leverage the powers of mapacho. In addition to the variety of applications, how much you consume will also determine your experience. While each form of the medicine has different effects, here are some of the most frequently reported sensations:

- Enhanced senses
- Boosted energy, uplifted mood, and improved focus
- Induced visions and connections with the inner self and surroundings
- Feeling more grounded
- Ease of anxiety or confusion
- All the purgative effects as well, including sweating, vomiting, diarrhea, and the expulsion of phlegm

These sensations can last from a few minutes to several hours. As you can tell, mapacho is a master plant medicine in its own right, and a valuable ally on the healing path of ayahuasca.

Ambil & Mambé

People are often quite chatty after an ayahuasca ceremony and it is not uncommon that participants congregate to share experiences and takeaways. It is definitely the most fun happy hour I have ever attended! I started to notice some people's teeth were covered in this weird green gunk. They were not bothered and didn't even cover their mouths when they laughed. To me, it looked like they hadn't brushed their teeth in twenty years.

What is Ambil & Mambé

Ambil and mambé are both sacred plant medicines that are often used in combination, after an ayahuasca ceremony and on their own outside of ceremony. These plant medicines originate with the Amazonian indigenous cultures who have been working and praying with these plants for thousands of years.

Ambil is the Divine Masculine, or Father Spirit. It is derived from tobacco and is prepared by taking the leaves and cooking them in fresh water for hours until it is a very thick dark paste. Ambil is sometimes referred to as the blood of tobacco and has a nutty and sweet flavor, but can also be slightly bitter. It contains vegetal salts (usually from the ash of a burnt palm trunk) which are rich in health-giving minerals. Ambil is completely legal in the United States and other parts of the Western world.

Mambé is the Divine Feminine, and translates to "the tongue of God" or "word of life". It is an ultra-fine green powder made from ground up toasted coca leaves (not to be confused with cocoa, which will be discussed later) and often mixed with the ash of burnt leaves of the yarumo tree. Mambé, sometimes referred to as Mama Coca is a sacred plant medicine, mainly used to aid in sound health and right words, thoughts and conduct. It can clarify awareness, and harmonize man with man and men with nature and the cosmos.

While mambé is legal in most of Central and South America, to this day, there is great confusion about the differences between coca and cocaine. Mambé is mistakenly thrown into the same category of cocaine because it is derived from coca leaves. It appears the legislature forgot that cocaine also includes sulfuric acid, acetone, gasoline, diesel, sodium carbonate, potassium permanganate, and cement. Oh, and cocaine is also a deadly substance, not an age-old plant that has been used for its medicinal and spiritual properties for more than 8,000 years. Sadly, it is still illegal to bring coca into the United States and much of the Western world for any purpose. Coca, in any of its forms, including as mambé, tea or whole leaves, are considered a Schedule II substance.

How Ambil & Mambé are Consumed

When there is a request for guidance, an opportunity to share, or a desire to receive knowledge from the plant, animal, or spirit worlds, these two beautiful plant medicines can be consumed together as a vehicle to carry our prayers to the Creator. They are often used among the tribes to clarify and sweeten communication, as it helps us to be more sincere in our dealings with one another and use intention and awareness in our words.

Ambil and mambé are generally used before or after an ayahuasca ceremony, but like most plant medicines, they can be used anytime as a tool for spiritual connection, improved communication, and writing. (I have had them tucked in my mouth while writing the majority of this book!). Mambé is a stimulant, so it is best not to consume before bed.

To receive ambil and mambé:

- Place a small amount of ambil on your pinkie and offer prayer and gratitude. The pinky finger serves as a reminder to pray for ourselves as well as offer gratitude to the medicine, for our blessings, and for the love we receive.

- Following your prayers and offering to ambil, you can place the ambil on your tongue or coat your top and bottom gums with it, and swish it around in your mouth. Ambil will cause an increase in saliva which you will use with the mambé.

- After you consume the ambil, put a 1/2 teaspoon of mambé in a spoon and offer your prayers and gratitude.

- Following your offering to mambé, gently pull your cheek away from your teeth, and place the powder deep in the back corner pocket of your bottom jawline. While it is okay to swallow a little mambé that may be on your tongue or teeth, the goal is not to swallow or eat it just yet.

- The concoction of ambil and mambé will slowly absorb through the mucus lining of your mouth, generally taking thirty minutes to an hour. After a period of time, you can swallow the mambé that doesn't get absorbed, or simply spit it out.

When in prayer, traditionally both medicines are used in combination, however each can be used on its own.

Ambil used individually will help realign the chakras, aid in reducing anxiety, ground you emotionally, and encourage positive, insightful conversation. It can increase energy and mental clarity, and aid in the quitting of smoking cigarettes. Ambil is the empowerment of male energy and is a wound healer when applied externally to cuts and wounds, as it is antibacterial and antiseptic. To use ambil on its own, simply place about a lentil size amount in the mouth along the gum line and allow it to slowly dissolve. Swallowing too much ambil over time can be taxing to the liver, so please consume with intention and try to not swallow, but rather absorb the plant medicine through your gums.

How Does Ambil & Mambé Feel

Like Sonny and Cher, Batman and Robin, or tofu burgers and fries, these two are another example of the perfect pairing. While on their own, each can be incredibly beautiful and effective, when used together they create a symbiosis you will be grateful for.

When slowly absorbed through the mucus lining of the mouth, ambil and mambé provide the following benefits and sensations:[8]

- Encouragement of positive, insightful conversation
- Wakefulness; a sharpening of one's concentration and short-term memory
- Slight numbness in the area where applied
- A dampening of appetite
- Reduction of altitude sickness
- A subtle "high" or feeling of general happiness
- Realignment of the chakras
- Emotional grounding
- Endurance of long work days, for driving long distances, or for needed concentration over many hours, because it is a stimulant

(continued…)

- Healing of the father wound and alignment of the divine masculine within (Ambil alone)
- Healing of wounds with its antibacterial and antiseptic properties (Ambil alone)

Mambé is also a wonderful vitamin supplement. Several studies analyzed the nutrition characteristics of the coca leaf. One in particular was a 1975 Harvard study (Nutritional Value of Coca Leaf, Duke, Aulick, Plowman) that found the leaves contain vitamin A, B1, B2, B6, C, D (trace amounts), and E, as well as calcium, copper, iron, magnesium, potassium, phosphorus, and zinc among other things.

Cacao

When we hear the word cacao, most of us think of the sweet, processed chocolate that line the check-out aisles of our grocery stores. While a lovely Godiva truffle may stem from cacao, it is not the unprocessed raw beautiful sacred plant medicine which possesses so many powerful physical, emotional and spiritual healing properties. Like a warm cup of love, cacao is a potent energetic medicine used in combination alongside other plant medicines, as well as on its own.

What is Cacao

The word cacao originally comes from the Mayan words Ka'kau and Chokola'j, which translates as "to drink chocolate together".[9] Cacao is also said to be translated by certain tribes as "heart blood," or "food of the Gods", each emphasizing the importance and power the plant possesses.

Cacao has been used by various cultures for more than 5,000 years as a medicine to heal physical, mental and spiritual illnesses.[10] Cacao ceremonies originate all the way back to Mayan and Aztec traditions in Central and South America, and were used for spiritual, medicinal and ceremonial purposes for inner awakening and creative guidance.

Cacao is not cocoa, so let me explain the difference.[11] Cacao is the tree as well as the raw, unrefined bean. The term cocoa is the bean after it has been roasted, and then processed into consumable items like the chocolate you will find in packages, nibs, liquor, cocoa powder, or butter. You may notice a percentage on cocoa packages, which refers to the total cocoa content within. The higher the percentage, the more cocoa and subsequently less sugar, the more bitter and healthier it is.

Conversely, cacao is the natural and unprocessed seed of the cacao tree. After the seed is winnowed and processed, and the butter is removed, a highly concentrated natural fine powder remains.

Cacao contains a psychoactive ingredient called theobromine.[12] Theobromine is a bitter alkaloid and a mild stimulant. It has been shown to boost the immune system, lower blood pressure, decrease the risk of cardiovascular disease, and possibly reduce "bad" cholesterol and improve "good" cholesterol. Cacao is said to improve blood flow throughout the body, further supporting the heart. Cacao contains serotonin, which is shown to improve mood and decrease stress. That, with theobromine can be used to help symptoms of depression. Cacao also contains anandamide, a "bliss" chemical that produces a feeling of euphoria. Because these ingredients are contraindicated alongside ayahuasca, it is not recommended to consume cacao prior to ceremony.

How Cacao is Consumed

While a cacao ceremony is best in a group, you can have your own solo ceremony in the comfort of your own home. As with all plant medicines, know who you are buying cacao from. I recommend sourcing 100% pure ceremonial grade cacao.

When starting your relationship with cacao, consume a smaller amount so you can get acquainted with the medicine and understand how it interacts with your body. Too much cacao can cause nausea, constipation, headache, anxiety, increased urination, sleeplessness, and a fast heartbeat. I started with less than a tablespoon. Cacao has caffeine so beyond ceremonial purposes, it is best to consume it in the morning or during the day on a somewhat empty stomach. Do not consume cacao in combination with coffee.

To make a cacao brew:

- Simmer six to eight ounces of water, or the milk of your choice (I prefer oat) and one to two tablespoons of cacao.

- Because cacao can be a little bitter (it is medicine after all), you can add a teaspoon of honey to sweeten it. Do not add processed sugars or sugar substitutes.

- If you have rose water, you can add to further invoke love!

- As a lovely add on, dried lavender or a cinnamon stick can be added to your simmering cacao brew, which you will strain when it is ready.

As with any plant medicine, start by setting your intentions and offer gratitude. Find a quiet place to sit and contemplate your intentions, while you very slowly sip this magic.

How Does Cacao Feel

Where to start! Cacao has almost too many wonderful effects and benefits, including:

- Euphoria; deeper spiritual connection; bliss
- Open heart, connection to the love within us
- Feelings of relaxation and warmth
- Improved energy, mildly to very stimulating depending on how much consumed
- Increased blood flow to the brain, improving focus and memory
- Release of endorphins and dopamine, feel-good hormones resulting in feeling happier and more creative
- Increased clarity in the areas of love, purpose, intuitive abilities, career and personal growth
- Openings of awareness and improved workings of the mind, valued by many as a tool for meditation

Cacao also has a strong anti-stress and antidepressant effect, which is why it is perfect after an ayahuasca ceremony, acting like a salve to help relax and remove negative emotions and thoughts from our head, and improving overall well-being. Many people like to enjoy cacao as a creative aid for inspiration, useful for connecting with the Muse and entering the flow.

Cacao is not only a plant medicine, but it is a super food and one to be revered. Skip the java, and have yourself a cup of cacao instead!

Sananga

There is no orifice that escapes the plant medicine realm, even the eyes! When I first encountered sananga, no one told me to get ready for one of the most intense physical experiences, followed by a beautiful emotional encounter that I would subsequently sign up for again and again.

I heard about all the amazing physical and spiritual benefits of sananga so I did some research, bought a bottle from one of my trusted online sources, and eagerly awaited its arrival. Once in hand, I was immediately terrified and placed it in my refrigerator for over a month.

Mustering up the courage, I called upon my then 15-year-old son to administer the drops. I set my intentions, offered gratitude, and laid down to receive the medicine. He and I had absolutely no idea what was in store but upon request, he applied the drops. Once I opened my eyes for the medicine to drop in, I exclaimed "Holy cow, this is not sananga. This must be jalapeno pepper juice!"

The intensity of the pain was not something I had expected. I went to my tried-and-true breath and within a few minutes, the pain started to dissipate. What happened thereafter was beautiful and much to my son's relief, I immediately started to laugh. All the tension in my face and body eased. My mind felt crystal clear and I was able to contemplate things differently. I dropped into a meditative state for a significant time and understood why this medicine is so important and central in the plant medicine realm.

What is Sananga

It is unclear when sananga first appeared among the indigenous peoples of the Amazon jungle, but it is said to date back some 10,000 years.[13] Sananga is a sacred and powerful medicine that is derived from several plants and roots based on the tribe's tradition and lineage. Commonly though, it is made from the roots and bark of the Tabernaemontana undulata shrub, which is a milkwood species in the family Apocynaceae. These flowering plants are evergreen shrubs and small trees with leaves that have a milky sap, which is why it is called milkwood.

Sananga is traditionally administered as eyedrops by a Sanangueros. Some tribes use sananga to sharpen their vision for hunting at night, however it does much more than that. These powerful eye drops have a healing power that is more spiritual than physical. Sananga has the capacity to increase insight in the minds of those who use it. And who can't use a fresh perspective sometimes?

Sananga is commonly used in preparation for ayahuasca ceremonies due to its capacity to increase visual perception, enhance colors and remove unwanted energy. While sananga can temporarily cause an intense burning sensation for up to ten minutes, experienced practitioners feel the pain is an important part of the healing process. In my experience, my ayahuasca journeys are typically far more visual when sananga precedes the ceremony, so when it is offered, I absolutely always partake.

If you are considering cultivating a home practice, sananga is completely legal in the United States and in most parts of the world. Outside of an ayahuasca ceremony, sananga is a wonderful tool for meditation, grounding, relaxation, and deep sleep as it calms the central nervous system.[14]

Once you have gained a comfort with this plant medicine, buy it from a trusted source. The strength of each sananga blend can vary significantly, as some are far more potent than others, so be sure to ask questions from the source of your sananga. If you are very sensitive to pain or the sananga you receive is too strong, you can always dilute the medicine with saline solution or distilled water. Sananga must also be stored in the refrigerator and is only fresh for up to six months.

How to Receive Sananga

Based on my first experience, I highly recommend working with a trusted professional when receiving sananga for the first time.

To receive sananga:

- Recipients are asked to lie flat and keep their eyes closed. The Sananguero or facilitator will place one drop of the plant medicine in each corner of the eye.

- You will then be instructed to open both eyes simultaneously and blink, allowing the medicine to drop in.

- Time to buckle up buttercup. This is where it can get pretty intense! Immediately after the medicine drops in, you may feel extreme burning in and around your eyes. You can blink rapidly and roll your eyes to better distribute the medicine. You can use a tissue to pat the outside of your eyes, but do not rub them.

- You are encouraged to be still and simply breathe deeply into the discomfort until it dissipates in order to reap all of the benefits this plant medicine can offer.

If you wear contact lenses, make sure to take them out prior to receiving the drops. You will need to wait at least one hour before putting your lenses back in. Those who have artificial lenses or have had cataract surgery should not receive sananga.

If you are using sananga at home, find a quiet and calm space and set your intentions. It is ideal to have someone apply the drops for you, but you can receive sananga by yourself. Just place one drop in one open eye at a time. Be sure to place sananga in the second eye, no matter how it feels. Apply the drops at night before bed or before your seated meditation.

How Does Sananga Feel

Ok, so I think I have made it clear, most people feel intense stinging and pain in the eyes for an average of ten minutes after receiving sananga, along with some redness and slight swelling. A handful of recipients may not feel this pain as intensely, but they are uncommon. Aside from this obvious physical effect, you may feel the following:

- Stronger connection to spiritual realms; expanded consciousness
- Opening of the third eye
- Improved concentration, clearer mind, head rush
- Powerful sense of euphoria and lightness
- Sharpened physical and spiritual vision
- Increased mental insight, new perspective, fresh outlook
- Helps to activate and decalcify the pineal gland
- Clearing of negative energies
- Buzzing, vibration, or mild tinnitus in the ears
- Calming of the central nervous system, and therefore a great medicine to use as a meditation before bed

Sananga has not been widely studied in a clinical setting, but some data suggests that sananga can aid in the treatment of ocular diseases such as glaucoma and astigmatism. Sananga has been shown to be anti-inflammatory and effective in treating skin infections due to its antimicrobial properties, as well as having antifungal and antioxidant properties, which may prove effective in preventing cataracts and macular degeneration.

Vomitivo Ceremony

Yep, it is exactly as it sounds. Some tribes and retreat centers practice what is called a vomitivo ceremony prior to drinking ayahuasca. The word vomitivo refers both to a substance used to induce vomiting and to the instance in which the substance is employed. The purpose of the ceremony is to prepare and cleanse the body, stomach and intestinal track prior to working with ayahuasca, as well as clear any dense physical energies.

What Is Used in a Vomitivo Ceremony

There are many purgative plants used in a vomitivo ceremony, depending on the tribe. The two most commonly used are lemongrass tea and tobacco.

Lemongrass tea is an herbal tea made from dried leaves or stalks of the lemongrass plant known as Cymbopogon citratus, or hierba luisa. It is the same plant used to make lemongrass oil, and citronella candles, and as culinary herbs.[15] It is naturally caffeine free and in daily life can offer many health benefits. Lemongrass tea aids in digestion, is anti-inflammatory, and is a natural diuretic. It may help prevent infection that can harm digestion thanks to the presence of polyphenols and antioxidants. This tea carries light energy, so when introduced to our bodies, we naturally feel healthier and cleaner.

When using tobacco in a vomitivo ceremony, it is either boiled, cooled and served as a juice or it is soaked and eaten.

How To Consume the Purgative in a Vomitivo Ceremony

Vomitivo ceremonies are usually conducted the day prior to or on the first morning of your first ayahuasca ceremony. The vomitivo ceremony format is pretty straight forward. You are served a large glass or bowl of lemongrass tea, which you must drink as fast as possible. Immediately following, you are served either more liquid, or some tribes simply serve large quantities of warm water. Eventually, the body will want to be rid of all of this fluid via vomiting. Similarly, tobacco juice or the soaked tobacco is consumed until vomiting is induced.

How Does Vomitivo Feel

While this may initially sound absolutely awful, most people feel great following a vomitivo ceremony and do not regret participating. However, if this practice is concerning to you, know that not all facilities do vomitivo ceremonies so it is best to ask the retreat center before booking. I want to add, you may actually benefit by participating in a vomitivo ceremony with an open mind. While common sense is always a factor, I tend to trust the people that have been consuming ayahuasca for lineages.

While you may not feel great during a vomitivo ceremony, the following experiences are possible:

- Feeling clearer mentally
- Improved energy, lighter
- Feeling cleaner, healthier

Plant Medicines Conclusion

It is always exciting to learn about all of the resources which help me connect with nature and assist my spiritual journey. Rapé, mapacho, ambil, mambé, cacao, and sananga now share space in my medicine cabinet and I am so grateful for their wisdom and healing. With knowledge, patience, and practice, I really got my plant medicine groove on! Isn't it great to know you have so many options for healing and learning with these plant medicines?

Chapter 11
How Ayahuasca Heals

Until you make the unconscious conscious, it will rule your life and you will call it Fate.
Carl Jung

My favorite thing to do leading up to ceremony is to talk with other participants and learn about their history, and the reasons they came to the medicine. I keep a mental note of their body language, the pace and intensity of their words, and how they describe their stories. Following the ceremonies, I catch up with them to see what, if anything, has shifted. The transformation is typically incredible. It reminds me of those extreme makeover shows, but instead of a new hairstyle and new clothes, their aura is what received the upgrade.

If you are a chatterbox like me, you will come to learn there is an incredibly high preponderance of veterans, addicts and people with PTSD. As my relationship with the medicine grew deeper, and I learned of others' trauma, I began to understand why the medicine attracts this population in droves. The news is out that ayahuasca is an incredible option for healing such deep rooted and often misunderstood and disregarded pain.

There are many ways ayahuasca may assist in healing. How you will understand your healing with ayahuasca depends on your worldview, beliefs, and practices. In the West, many are approaching the topic through scientific studies of measurable changes to the brain and reported changes from participants in formalized studies.[1] Others are more drawn to the study of psychology because ayahuasca takes us deep into the psyche where we encounter highly meaningful memories, feelings, stories, and themes that speak to our life experiences. Finally, many who sit with ayahuasca will walk away with a renewed spiritual perspective. Let's explore these frameworks in light of how ayahuasca works Her healing magic.

The Scientific View of Healing

The traditional Western scientific approach of observing and measuring material reality has only gone so far in the study of ayahuasca, but there have been some initial conclusions about how the medicine changes the brain.

There are numerous studies demonstrating how ayahuasca increases activity in the brain, specifically the right hemisphere including the anterior insula and the anterior cingulate and frontal-medial cortex.[2] These areas are responsible for somatic awareness, emotional arousal, feelings, and processing of emotional information. Additionally, ayahuasca increases activity in the left hemisphere's amygdala and parahippocampal gyrus structures which also play a role in emotional arousal and memory. This enables ayahuasca to make repressed memories conscious and for the recipient to re-experience emotions associated with them, enabling one to reprocess these memories in more constructive ways and with more potential for healing.

Other studies have shown that ayahuasca helps recipients shift from their brain's default mode network ("DMN")" which is active when engaging in self-reflection, self-other dynamics, and remembering the past and thinking about the future.[3] By freeing us from the rigid patterning of the DMN, ayahuasca opens us to new perspectives and ways of being that we could not access before. Indeed, participants report "decentering" after their ceremony, which means they have the ability to observe their thoughts with detachment. Decentering is a common trait among meditators as well, often seen as conducive to equanimity.

As Joe Dispenza discusses in his book, *Breaking the Habit of Being Yourself: How to Lose Your Mind and Create a New One*, the key to happiness may be releasing attachment to the patterned self, conditioned by past experiences and, instead, exist spontaneously fresh in the present moment. Ayahuasca seems to loosen our grip on the habitual self who suffers with the same-old depressive thoughts and feelings so that we may recreate ourselves on the ever-changing path of spiritual growth and evolution.

Other studies show that ayahuasca recipients demonstrate decreased anxiety and depression, more openness and optimism, and fewer tendencies toward addictive and harmful behavior.[4] These studies are a good start for the Western scientific community. However, to understand the healing benefits of ayahuasca, you must enter into the subjective and unmeasurable dimensions of the experience. The psychological and spiritual perspectives of healing will take us deeper in that regard.

The Psychological View of Healing

The plant medicine community talks quite a bit about "shadow work" and it is a very important concept to understand fully. The term shadow work was popularized by Carl Jung, a Swiss psychiatrist and psychoanalyst. Essentially, it is identifying the unconscious parts of the personality the conscious ego does not want to recognize or identify with. Jung states *"Unfortunately there can be no doubt that man is, on the whole, less good than he imagines himself or wants to be. Everyone carries a shadow, and the less it is embodied in the individual's conscious life, the blacker and denser it is. If an inferiority is conscious, one always has a chance to correct it. Furthermore, it is constantly in contact with other interests, so that it is continually subjected to modifications. But if it is repressed and isolated from consciousness, it never gets corrected."*[5]

The shadow is our dark side, the things that are repressed or ignored. This is not only personality traits we deem undesirable or unacceptable, but also trauma and conditioned beliefs. The shadow, when left unearthed and unexplored, can lead to undesired and unintended outcomes such as addictions and destructive behaviors, limited beliefs, ruined relationships, and the like. The work, then, is identifying and acknowledging these shadows, bringing that which is dark into the light. It is working with your unconscious mind to discover the shadow that suppresses a full, happy, and liberated life.

Ayahuasca loves to get into the depths of your shadow. It's Her thing, really. Now, while intuitively, you may want to run from this exposure, the work requires confrontation with the shadow, identifying what is brought to your attention, and liberating the vital energy trapped within. Be especially loving and kind with yourself during this process and know that She is a master at showing you how to accomplish this freedom. Be mentally prepared for this experience and be ready to embrace the opportunity for the learning and integration. You are so worth it.

What is Trauma?

The psychological approach to understanding ayahuasca's benefits centers on healing from trauma. From research, we know that traumatic instances create psychological-somatic complexes which alter our brains and nervous systems. A traumatic event is one that overwhelms the nervous system and the capacity of the mind to experience, understand, resolve, and integrate the event. Many extreme traumas come from sexual or physical assault, war, or other exceptional cases of violence or loss like losing a loved one, surviving a natural disaster or mass shooting, or being involved in a serious car accident. However, most people in the modern age have faced normalized childhood environments of stress, coercion, fear, punishment, blame, and other forms of subtle (or not-so-subtle) traumas.

What happens when we experience trauma that cannot be integrated?

When the experience is too much, we separate from it, shutting down the power supply to that region of our nervous system. From a depth-psychological perspective, the experience itself, complete with the memory, sensations, and feelings, is repressed into the unconsciousness. From the mind-body perspective, that area of the unconsciousness is contained in the body.

When we split off from our wholeness because of traumatic events or conditioning, we find ourselves in constant states of fight, flight, or freeze as the nervous system is stuck reacting as if the trauma is still occurring. Indeed, the amygdala, the brain's center for regulating the fear-response, is overactive in people suffering from unresolved trauma.[6] Such people suffer in a state of survival, repressing the original trauma and living as a split-off portion of the self.

In shamanic work, the splitting of the self is known as "soul loss". Some shamans believe soul loss occurs when a trauma causes a piece of the soul to depart into the underworld, leaving the "conscious self" feeling incomplete and lost.[7] An experienced shaman can journey to the underworld and perform "soul retrieval" to bring back the lost part of self to the traumatized person.

How Does Ayahuasca Help?

Ayahuasca brings full awareness to unresolved traumas by allowing repressed experiences to re-surface to be experienced fully and with complete awareness. The only way we can heal from these traumas is by re-experiencing, fully accepting, and integrating the original events. This healing often involves intense physical experiences as the sensations and emotions of the repressed traumas are fully felt. You may feel the dread you could not process fully as a child when you were afraid of your father's anger. You may feel the desolation of loneliness and despair when you thought your mother was abandoning you. You may feel the flare of rage as your inner child vents the frustrations of being repressed for so many years.

Finally, after feeling and feeling and feeling all that you have repressed for so long, you may find yourself fully open again, as you were when you were a child. In this space, your heart is no longer closed in protection, and you are now free to hold the experience with love. Tears of compassion may come as you forgive yourself and others. This experience re-writes the patterns of the nervous system and brain chemistry so you may live from a non-reactive point of view. By resolving the trauma, you cease living in the past and may enter fully into the present. Ayahuasca does even more. She also helps us make sense of life's experiences in a meaningful way. As you are feeling your repressed emotions, ayahuasca may also show you how your perpetrator was doing the best they could, or how your experience gave you knowledge and gifts that you can now use to help others. This reframing of the past is just as important as the emotional healing, as it may bring forth forgiveness or purpose.

The above forms of psychological and somatic healing create new patterns of neurological pathways in your brain. Thus, you become a new person, responding differently to stimuli, seeing yourself and the world in a new light, and being free now to continue your journey of growth.

The Buddha teaches that most people unconsciously follow their karmic conditioning, as seen in a story about a man and a horse. The horse is galloping quickly, and it appears that the man on the horse is going somewhere important. An alarmed passerby shouts, "Where are you going?" and the man, holding on for dear life, replies, "I don't know! Ask the horse!"

Sound familiar? This is also our story. The horse is habit energy or conditioned responses and for many, it pulls us unconsciously along our life's path often leaving us to feel powerless, exhausted, and unfulfilled. Many of us are riding that horse, and do not know why we do the things we do, feel the way we feel, or know where we are headed. Many of us do not even know where we want to be or how to feel joy anymore. We are not living our life's purpose in wondrous alignment and ayahuasca's gifts are to lift the veil on our actions and enact the birthright of joy.

Meditators know the goal of such practices is full awareness, a state akin to liberation from past patterns of conditioning so that we may respond rather than react to the present moment. Meditation, when practiced consistently over years, has the power to bring us deeper into the unconscious body-mind to experience and integrate past memories of trauma. Considering the cross-over between meditation and ayahuasca healing, it may be of great benefit for the ayahuasca participant to practice the same investigative awareness found in a deep meditative state. Other yogic and somatic-based modalities of healing are very useful as well when combined with ayahuasca. An overview of several practices is featured in Chapter 5.

The Spiritual View of Healing

Insights from the psychological-somatic view often brings us into the spiritual dimensions of healing and growth. Some find that spiritual learning comes after ayahuasca helps cleanse our bodies and creates order of the inner house. First things first: Clear out the old furniture, sweep and mop the floors, repaint the walls, and then the transpersonal journey of spirit may come through.

Who Are We?

Spirituality seeks answers to the questions such as who are we, where do we come from, why are we here, and where are we going. Eventually, we all ponder these questions, and it is better to do so earlier in life so that we may live with greater self-understanding and purpose.

Ayahuasca is also known as the "vine of the dead" or "vine of souls" because She shows us how life and death are inseparable. She guides us to who we truly are beyond the body-mind ego-self. On the spiritual journey with Her, you may enter into the transpersonal dimensions, recognizing you are not the identity you previously thought. Your name, gender, occupation, possessions, and whole personality may indeed dissolve as you expand beyond the physical realm. You may find yourself in a more-real-than-real experience of merging with the entire cosmos, or what many would say is "God or Goddess," "The Universe," "Great Spirit," "Mind or Consciousness," or "The Absolute."

Such a mystical experience can transform your life. This awakening often carries over beyond the ayahuasca ceremony, orienting us to a sacred way of living honoring the aliveness of all things. When we see and experience the universal spirit, we will then act with reverence. Or at the least, try!

From recognizing the spiritual oneness of all of which we are a part, we find healing. The word "health" comes from the etymological meaning of "wholeness", to be healed is to feel and know oneself as part of life.[8] This applies on social, natural, and cosmic or spiritual levels. The integration of mind and body, which is so important for deep psychological-somatic healing, brings us to wholeness. Thus healed, the self connects with the world fresh and unfiltered, communing with nature and other people. We see ourselves as not separate from Mother Nature and our communities, but as part of it all. Research and experience show that alienation from nature and community are major causes of addiction and disease, so returning to communion with both is a major boon for health and the enjoyment of life.

The Shipibo people of the Amazon have an intriguing view on how ayahuasca brings us back to wholeness. They learn songs from the medicine which align their bodies and minds with the music of nature. From their perspective, the Universe is being sung into creation. Every plant is singing its song, vibrating its unique medicine into being. When we become traumatized and separated from nature (both without and within), then we lose touch with the songs of the Earth and cosmos. Ayahuasca can play Her music through us, realigning us with the music of creation.

What Is the Meaning of Life?

If we do not find meaning in life, we suffer. By reconnecting us to our spiritual nature, ayahuasca brings meaning to our lives. When we see ourselves as a part of everything, our instinct is to merge our creative and loving flow into the greater evolutionary play. This orientation of serving life saves us from despair and apathy. We may also find through our ayahuasca journey that we are here for a specific purpose, and that our entire life has been guided to this very point in preparation for our offerings.

Indeed, many find deeper understanding about who they are and why they are here. This knowing may be hard to communicate or justify, but it often does not require explanation. There can be a deep knowing beyond words. Discovering your life's purpose or mission can lift you from hopelessness to inspiration.

In short, there may be a thousand varieties of the spiritual experience encountered on ayahuasca journey, and a variety of interpretations for each person. Most importantly, it is your experience and not what someone else told you. Your journey of spiritual enlightenment is yours alone.

Becoming the Sovereign

Another element of spiritual awakening is becoming the sovereign of your life. Spiritually, we are like the king or queen, wandering our lands with amnesia. We forget that we are children of God, so to speak, inseparable from the ever-present mysterious Consciousness which creates the cosmos. In the forgetting, we acquiesce to smaller roles, pretend to be a "good girl" or a successful investment banker, or whatever else. The spiritual journey's goal is to come home to the truth of Self, to the throne in the heart where we may sit as the sovereign. When we are centered, our lives are ordered through the harmonizing frequencies of our true essence. When we take our place on the throne, the kingdom becomes ordered by the Law of the cosmos, or by the Tao, as Lao-Tze would say.

When we become the sovereign of our lives, we become the creator of our lives. Creation is the play of Spirit. We are aspects of the Creator Mind that come to play in this Universe. We are here to co-create the world, and ayahuasca empowers us to perform this task with duty and grace.

What About Addiction?

If you attend a few ayahuasca circles, you will hear people share stories about how ayahuasca helped them overcome addictions. Even very serious addictions, which mainstream medicine struggles to remedy, are frequently resolved through a committed healing path with ayahuasca. Why is this? How could a visionary healing plant medicine from the Amazon help people transcend opioid, alcohol or life-long tobacco addictions, eating disorders, and pornography addictions? The answer is found in why these addictions started in the first place.

Maybe you have heard of the rat park studies on addiction.[9] First, a scientist put rats in isolated cages stocked with two water sources. One of pure water and the other laced with morphine. As predicted, the rats became addicted to the morphine water and drank it to death.

However, Dr. Bruce Alexander was not satisfied with the first study's methods. Dr. Alexander thought, "What if we designed this experiment in a context where the rats could find other opportunities for fulfillment?" So he designed a mini-rat park complete with nature, exercise wheels, and socializing among the rats. But what about the drugs? They were there too. As with the first experiment, half the water sources were pure and half were laced with morphine. What do you think happened? Did the rats drink the morphine water and become addicted, spiraling down to their deaths?

No. The rats tried the drug water but were more interested in socializing, running on the wheels, and otherwise being free rats in the park.

Humans are similar. If we are isolated from nature and community, working meaningless jobs to survive, and offered addictive opportunities, we try to assuage the pain of isolation with drugs and distraction. People do not become addicted because "that's human nature;" they become addicts because they are living in constant emotional pain. Worse still, many people live in these dehumanizing contexts while bearing the crosses of more extreme traumas. When the underlying traumas are resolved, then the addictions dissipate, sometimes, as reported, without effort.

There is no one-size-fits-all answer for how ayahuasca helps us heal from addictions. For many though, ingrained patterns of trauma need to be released. Remember that the "trauma brain" is always operating on high-alert to defend the self from experiencing repressed emotions. That state is like the princess and the pea. No matter how much comfort we try to find, we will always face the nagging pain of not being at peace.

The End of the Ceremony, The Healing

Michael Pollan shares Don Victor's theory of trauma in his book, *This is Your Mind on Plants:* "When any part of your body has been affected by destructive energies or trauma, the heart will close down to protect itself. A closed heart will not heal. It will not express its feelings. The mind becomes more active because the heart's not feeling anymore. The mind will go into the past or it will go into the future, which doesn't really exist, and it will get stuck in a chaos, between remembering the past and trying to go into the nonexistent future. And it will lose the gift of life, which is to live and be present in the moment. That is why another word for a gift is a present."[10]

The healing journey of ayahuasca is just that--a journey. It is a process, not a one-and-done experience. You went and did it, purged in a bucket and now you can go home smelling like roses, right? Maybe. But more likely you are just beginning your healing journey after your first time sitting with ayahuasca. What our dear Grandmother Ayahuasca does is give us the option of living a healing life. After the ceremony, it is time for you to do the work of embodying the lessons you learned with the medicine. Learning never ends in life. Healing never ends either. Nor does awakening to greater wisdom. The point is not to reach an end point, but to be free to evolve and play the game, dance the dance, and be who you are. The next chapter on integration takes us deeper into this topic of continuing the process with ayahuasca after the ceremony.

Chapter 12
What to Expect After Ceremony:
Integration, Healing & Your New Beginning

We shall not cease from exploration
And the end of all our exploring
Will be to arrive where we started
And know the place for the first time
- T.S. Eliot

In the ayahuasca community, there is a lot of conversation about integration and its importance when working with the medicine. While the word carries a lot of different meanings, integration is the process of consciously receiving insights and then translating them into direct action to benefit from this new information and grow into new ways of living aligned with our true nature and in harmony with the rest of life.

Wait, what? I went through all of that, and there's follow up homework? Yes, as the saying goes, there is more to a ceremony than "showing up and throwing up"!

Integration is the single most important element in working with the medicine, and is essential to allow for the healing experienced as a result of the ceremony to take root in our lives. While the mysterious ways of ayahuasca cannot be predicted and will not clear all trauma in a single ceremony, the practice of integration is very powerful and can enhance and further strengthen that experience. This is true for all psychedelics, but especially ayahuasca, as She often tells a story that can be cryptic and misunderstood if not thoroughly examined.

For some, this work is deep and can take months if not years of exploration. Follow-up integration is necessary to understand your ayahuasca experience, elaborate on the details, process how it felt, and identify the patterns in your life. It takes patience, ego strength, emotional wisdom, and a strong commitment to growth to work through what has been released and opened.

Below are suggestions for some practices and intentions that will support your integration process. The most important thing is that your learning path with ayahuasca is yours and yours alone. Everyone may have an opinion or advice for you, but you have the direct line to your higher wisdom and to ayahuasca as well. You had a unique journey with Her that only you can know and understand. Study your experience with deep contemplation.

Reflect on what you learned. Practice what She showed you about yourself. And keep the dialogue going with Her. She will continue to be a presence in your life if you keep the line open.

As a final word before delving into the integration framework, I want to underscore that your preparation for ayahuasca will be most important for ensuring a smooth and productive post-ceremony integration. If you prepare well, treating the process as one of the most important moments of your life, then you will get the most out of the ceremony and will naturally continue the process afterward.

Presence as a Daily Practice

A simple practice of presence in your daily life can assist you in all other integration practices. In an ayahuasca ceremony, we are brought deeper into ourselves, into the heart center, the meat and bones of our bodies, and into the visionary space of the third eye and higher mind. The love you found in your heart center and the tears of forgiveness that you cried was not ayahuasca, it was you. She opened the door to yourself and led you through by the hand (either gently if you went willingly or She pulled you kicking and screaming). I believe what ayahuasca wants is for us to continue the process of returning home to our true self.

To continue the homecoming, you may wish to practice a simple form of presence. What is it like for you right now as you read this? Start by connecting with the sensations in your feet. Now briefly scan your entire body, moving up through your legs, torso, chest, arms, shoulders, and face, noting any tension you are holding. Just observe it. Notice your breathing. Just observe it. As you breathe, allow the tension in your body to release. You do not have to do anything else. Just observe the experience of being you in this moment.

There are many variations of this meditative practice. Some people sit on a cushion with their spines straight to allow the body to relax in a state of alert wakefulness. You can also lay flat on your back in your bed or on a yoga mat, or sit in a chair. There really is no wrong way to tune in to your present moment. The important thing is that at least once per day (and ideally twice) you find time to practice presence. The first thing in the morning and the last thing before sleep are good times to aim for.

Last, your breath is your best friend. You always have your breath to connect you to the present moment. You are here. You are in the now. Breathing in, I am here. Breathing out, I am in the now.

Life as Ceremony: Get Ready to MC!

While feeling the effects of ayahuasca, you may find your emotional sensitivity greatly magnified. A stray thought, word, or judgment may send you tumbling into chaos, while a blessing may catapult you into tears of gratitude. When you stand to walk to the bathroom, your legs may feel wobbly so you mindfully take every step with careful attention. The last thing you want to do in ceremony is to rush!

Ayahuasca reminds us of how to live in the present moment, where life truly happens. The present moment is the only place where we may be the creators of our lives, "masters" of our ceremony. The Master of Ceremony is one who creates an existence through the intentional use of words and the power of one's presence. If we are lost in the past, feeling regret or guilt, then we miss out on creating this moment and the future. If we fret about the future, the same thing occurs: The present is lost.

Integration means to create your new life with a fresh perspective. You are not here to be defined by what your fifth-grade teacher said to you. You are not here to act out what is acceptable according to your culture. You are here to be you! Completely and authentically you! To do that you must be present and live with intention. Watching your words. Watching the "why" behind what you choose to say and do, and how you feel.

The post-ceremony integration process therefore asks you to evaluate yourself and your life in a deeper way. What are your values? What is your plan? If you do not have a plan, you may find yourself part of someone else's plan. Integration and becoming the master of your life -- your truest ceremony -- means self-inquiry. Who am I? What do I care about? What meaning do I want my life to have? How will I help myself? How will I help others?

As Socrates said, "The unexamined life is not worth living." One thing that ayahuasca will not ever let us do is go through Her ceremony without examining our lives.

Diet

Here is the scenario: You had a great ceremony weekend. It was challenging but wow, you worked through old pains, released negative beliefs and self-images, and now you feel great. You are buzzing with energy because your channels have been opened and cleared. You are aligned with yourself, standing tall with your shoulders relaxed and heart open. You feel on top of the world. As you hug your fellow ayahuasca brothers and sisters goodbye, you think there is no way you will ever not feel like this in the future.

Two weeks later you are, as some would say, "a mess." You feel heavy and blocked. Tired and foggy-headed. Irritable. Swarmed with self-defeating thoughts. Pulled toward the old habits of comfort—alcohol, TV, sugar, masturbation, or whatever else is your cup of escape tea.

Do not fret! The path of healing and learning is long and never a straight line. You may swirl around the spiral, dancing two steps forward and one step back. I equate this feeling to that of a snow globe. Ayahuasca shook that globe around during your ceremony so you can examine that which creates your physical, emotional and spiritual life. And now that you are returning to life, the snow begins to settle. This is completely normal and you are going to be okay. You can settle into equanimity and aid in the integration with careful intention and a dash of discipline, especially two to four weeks following an ayahuasca ceremony. This is a good time to be gentle and kind with yourself.

Hopefully you are already well versed on the dieta from the pre-ceremony preparation. If you skipped that section, it may be a good time to visit the material and really connect with it. Maintaining alignment with the dieta following ceremony is especially important. Over time, you may find a version of the dieta that you effortlessly choose to maintain simply because it makes you feel good. That's the thing about cleaning up the temple of the body: That big dish of ice cream probably won't feel the same way that it used to. Suddenly, there is a knowing that indigestion is a sign of imbalance and it becomes tolerable.

The post-ceremony dieta is similar to the pre-ceremony dieta, but you will notice it is a different process. With the higher sensitivity and intelligence of the medicine in your body and energetic field, you may be able to move into more of a feeling-based dance with your consumption choices. The more intention you put into the pre-ceremony dieta, the easier it will be to follow the dieta following ceremony.

Lastly, be aware that diet extends far beyond eating food. Humans are in a constant state of consumption, including our environments, the energies of the people that surround us, the information that we are listening to and believe come from trusted sources, and of course social media. Our minds have the big task of deciding how to use this information, and without tremendous awareness, the consumer may be unknowingly affected.

Be in a state of constant curiosity following ceremony, and ask yourself, "Does this environment make me feel at peace? Do these people nurture my desire to be authentic? Does watching the news negatively affect me, especially first thing in the morning, before even starting my day? Does reading crime fiction books before bed affect how I sleep?" Be sure to consume only what nourishes you. The rest, you can say, "No thank you, not for me any longer."

Joy: Follow Your Bliss

Ayahuasca ceremonies seem so serious, don't they? All this business about healing and growing, evolving and awakening, being the redeemer for your family lineage, and on and on and on. Now try this on for size: **What if we are here on Earth simply to be happy and love?** What if this is all, as they say, a song and a dance?

You only need to look to the Hindu God Shiva for inspiration. He is in a constant dance, united with his Goddess Shakti, creating the Universe together through their play. But much like our beautiful Grandmother Ayahuasca, He is a cosmic destroyer of negative presences such as evil, ignorance, and death which allows for positive re-creation.

Of course, in life there are always moments of sadness and sorrow, and I am not suggesting suppressing these emotions. Honor what is present and let go of your "should-be" judgements. But when you are free from the sadness and sorrow, dance, sing, be playful, be happy and laugh! Life can absolutely be a celebration. One of the best ways to heal from the past is to immerse yourself in joy and positivity.

Sir Isaac Newton taught us that an object at rest tends to stay at rest, and an object in motion tends to stay in motion. This most certainly holds true for our thoughts and feelings. By changing the way we think about someone or something, this then becomes a new force that can help us change the direction of our lives. Breaking the cycle of limiting or conditioned thoughts frees us and can change the direction of our lives.

So let go of the shame, anger, prejudice, and the like so you can have more capacity for love and growth. Follow your bliss! Even if it is just ten minutes a day to nurture yourself and fulfill your soul, over time, this may lead you to a life more aligned with your joyful pursuits. The things that light you up reflect the truth of who you are. Anytime we follow a path of truth and love, the Universe conspires to help us. Start with pursuing your joy and watch your life shift.

Find Your Tribe

There is no doubt we are social creatures who need and are here for each other. The medicine is all about communion and knowing thyself in sacred relationship with all others. One of the best things you can do for optimal integration is maintain connection to others on the same wavelength.

You may choose to attend weekly online integration calls or live meetings, knowing from direct experience that even just one meeting a week can go a long way. Sometimes I drag myself to these meetings, and when it is over, I am usually quite delighted to have learned new tools I can incorporate into my integration practice and daily life. Additionally, hearing other people's stories helps normalize my own experiences! Other healing and growth groups are likely available within range of your home as well. Check out women's or men's circles where people come together to share and support each other in their life journeys.

Meditation, prayer, or chanting groups can also be good sources of spiritual community.

Also consider finding (or even organizing) regular ceremonial circles. You do not need plant medicines to have a ceremony. Rather, you just need a space, the intention, a small group of people, and a plan for simple intentional activities or rituals to perform. For instance, at a fire ceremony each person can write down intentions or prayers on paper and then offer it to the fire (or speak intentions into small twigs and offer them to the fire).

A cacao ceremony can easily be incorporated into any ceremonial circle, enhancing heart opening, creativity, and healing. Bonus points for sitting in ceremony with cacao during the full moon! Consider buying some high-quality ceremonial-grade cacao and pass around a cup of love for your participants to enjoy and reflect.

If you set the intention for finding more community in alignment with your healing and growth process, you will find it. As your social circle shifts to reflect your true self, you will find yourself nourished in relationships that are right for you.

Ask the Right Questions

Process your ayahuasca experience within a day or so of ceremony by asking yourself questions. Life gets so busy and often we are launched back into the daily grind without really capturing everything that was experienced in ceremony. By asking pointed questions, you will develop a framework for the experience, which will help you determine how ayahuasca has helped you and if you plan on consuming again in the future.

These questions may be helpful following each ayahuasca ceremony:

1. Describe your journey in as much detail as possible. Take note of any physical sensations, mental experiences, emotional experiences, spiritual experiences, epiphanies, and visions you had during and following your ceremony.

2. What have you learned from your ayahuasca journey?

3. What has or will change as a result of your ayahuasca journey?

4. In what ways will you live life differently moving forward?

5. How would you rate the intensity of your experience?

6. How much medicine did you consume?

7. Did you consume more than once?

8. Were you comfortable with the intensity of your experience?

9. Do you believe you will drink ayahuasca again? Why or why not?

10. If you believe you will drink ayahuasca again, would you drink more or less?

Don't worry if you cannot remember everything from the experience. You may have received healing and incredible amounts of information which can be intense. Incorporating the gifts that you received can take days, weeks, and sometimes even months to assemble all the details. As time goes on, you may receive more clarity about your journey.

After the Ceremony Recap and Additional Resources

Presence, be the master of ceremony, diet, joy, and finding others. These are a sampling of what may assist you as you integrate your experience. Again, you will know what is right for you based on your on-going conversation with ayahuasca and your Higher Self or Spirit. Listening and applying whatever insights and wisdom flows from the experience may be the very essence of integration. An unnamed Eastern master had thoughts on this: "Enlightenment is doing the appropriate thing in the appropriate moment." In other words, practice listening in receptivity so that you can feel and know what to do in each moment, trusting the instincts that arise from being present.

This chapter suggested some main areas of focus to support receptive presence. Here are a few more ways to support integration:

- Acknowledgment journal. Write messages of self-love and acknowledgment of your efforts, growth, and victories.
- Reflection journal. Reflect on your experiences.
- Connect and work with an entheogen or integration coach.
- Work with a good therapist or healer.

(continued...)

- Get into nature as much as possible.
- Move your body. Yoga, stretching, hitting the gym, walking, running, Qigong, whatever works for you, but definitely move every day.
- Create. Part of following your joy is to allow yourself time to freely create for no other reason than creation.
- Read, watch, or listen to media that reinforces your path.
- Pay attention to your dreams. Start a dream journal. Observe the messages, symbols, and themes from your dreams. Ayahuasca will speak through your dreams for weeks, months, and even years if you want to continue the dialogue with Her.
- Pray. Keep praying to ayahuasca or God for support. Prayer in this way is a form of humbling and thus opening yourself to receive the blessings of support from Spirit.

With a solid post-ceremony plan and dedication, you can handle the work of your life. When we sit with ayahuasca, we are not separate from our lives. Rather, we more deeply enter into the essence of who we are, and learn how to live with freedom and intention.

After ceremony, it is time to carry the medicine of your truth and love into your world. What that looks like depends on the unique contours of your life. Just like when you sit with ayahuasca, if you show up with the right attitude and intention for healing, then your life will more and more become aligned with the highest good.

I'm so incredibly excited for you! Be safe on your journey and remember, you are never alone in the dark wherever She takes you.

Chapter 13
This Is the End...Or Is It?

Anna Freud was a psychoanalyst who continued the legacy of her father, Sigmund Freud. She famously said, "When an error becomes collective, it acquires the strength of a truth." I am confident I provided you with factual information and experiential truths about the benefits of plant medicine. I continue to have these important conversations with those who are interested in learning about ayahuasca to quell the misinformation and misunderstanding of this sacred medicine.

I believe this book is valuable, not necessarily because of my efforts but because of my spiritual brigade, the many teachers who have taught me along the way, making me who I am and providing the contents of my experience. I hope you feel more informed and can navigate this decision more effectively. Making the decision to drink ayahuasca can be as easy as breathing or the most challenging decision of your life.

If you fall in love with ayahuasca or any of the plant medicines as I did, you may find your state of mind is always in a beautiful ceremony.

I hope you find your healing. Because when you heal, I heal. And the world can use so much more of that.

Definitions

You are going to hear a lot of new terminology as you enter into this alternative world of healing. Of course, the following list of definitions is not conclusive, but these are certainly the most prevalent terminologies. Spend some time getting acquainted with these words so you do not get taken by surprise and can communicate effectively.

Shaman

The most important terminology is how we refer to the experienced healer who leads the ayahuasca ceremony. There are several ways to refer to someone who serves ayahuasca and oversees and guards a ceremony. Some general terminology, in addition to shaman, includes:

- Ayahuasquero, Ayahuasquera
- Curandero, Curandera (not all are shamans)
- Maestro, Maestra
- Taita
- Vegetalista

A'ho

You may hear people saying "A'ho" to each other in and around an ayahuasca ceremony. A'ho may be akin to namaste in the yoga community. However, this word does not come from the Amazonian jungle medicine world, rather its origins are Native American. Consider following the shaman's lead when using the term A'ho, as it may be better suited for Native American plant medicine ceremonies.

Agua de Florida ("Water of the Flowers", or Florida Water)

A fragrant water/cologne used for cleansing, usually administered via a spray, poured into the participants hands, or applied by the shaman via soplar. Agua de Florida is alcohol based, and includes a large variety of healing herbs and flowers.

Ambil

A thick dark paste derived from tobacco; often used in combination with mambé. See Chapter 10.

Banisteriopsis Caapi

Ayahuasca vine; combined with Psychotria viridis for an ayahuasca brew.

Cacao

The natural and unprocessed seed of the Cacao tree, which is winnowed, processed, and turned into a natural fine powder. Not to be confused with cocoa. See Chapter 10.

Chacruna

Also known as Psychotria viridis, the leaves in an ayahuasca brew which contain dimethyltryptamine (DMT).

Chakapa / Shakapa

A bundle of dry leaves that when shaken produces a rattle-like sound; often used in an ayahuasca ceremony as a traditional cleansing technique, as well as for rhythmic accompaniment to singing.

Chumbe

A ceremonial belt is typically woven from yarn, cotton, or wool providing protection to power centers and locks in the powerful energy that travels through the navel. Traditionally, women wear the medicine belt through their menstruation or during pregnancy. Men wear the medicine belt during hunting and traditional ceremonies.

Entheogen

A chemical substance, typically of plant origin, that is ingested to produce a non-ordinary state of consciousness for religious or spiritual purposes.

Icaros

A song, chant or whistle that calls upon plant spirits. Icaros are the principal tools that shamans use to manage and direct the energy and flow of an ayahuasca ceremony. More than just songs, an icaros is an invocation that channels plant spirit medicine. They are learned through rigorous plant dietas, and are taught directly by the spirits or learned from one's teacher. See "Music in Ceremony" in Chapter 7.

Limpia

A limpia, or spiritual cleansing, is performed by the shaman prior to and often during ceremony which helps balance or rid the person of certain physical and spiritual energies acquired during their lifetime. Shamans perform limpias in a variety of ways, including singing beautiful icaros (tribal songs), applying lotions, clicking, whistling, and other advanced techniques aimed to help the participant.

Maloca

A round building with tall, conical-shaped thatch roofing, built in an open-air style with mosquito netting around the perimeter. Traditionally where ayahuasca is consumed, but may also function as community gathering spaces.

Mambé

An ultra-fine green powder made from ground up toasted coca leaves; often used in combination with ambil. See Chapter 10.

Mapacho

Nicotiana rustica, or tobacco. Commonly administered as a medicine plant in and of itself and is widely used as a complement to ayahuasca ceremonies and healing. See Chapter 10.

Plant Dieta (or simply "Dieta")

A specialized diet followed for a period of time to prepare for an ayahuasca ceremony. See Chapter 4.

Psychotria Viridis

The leaves in an ayahuasca brew which contain dimethyltryptamine (DMT); also known as chacruna or yagé.

Purge
The release or expulsion of traumas, or bad energies. For types of purges, see Chapter 9.

Sananga
A plant medicine administered via eye drops. See Chapter 10.

Santo Daime
A spiritual movement originating in Brazil that involves the taking of ayahuasca as a sacrament. Santo Daime can also refer to the type of ayahuasca served.

Sacred Snuff (a.k.a. Rapé or Hapé)
Pronounced "ra-peh" or "ha-peh"; a complex blend of pulverized Amazonian medicinal plants, trees, leaves, seeds, and other sacred ingredients administered by blowing in the nose via a kuripe (for self-administration) or via a tepi (for administration by the shaman, or other qualified individual). See Chapter 10.

Soplar or Sopla
A blowing action used by the shaman to transfer or clear energy. Also referred to as Camay. Typically done with Agua de Florida, mapacho, or other plant medicines.

Venteada

A one-on-one personal icaro. Venteadas are given for a variety of reasons, including to induce healing or purging, calm one's mareación (the collective effects of an ayahuasca experience), open visions, ground, and for protection. Ventear is a Spanish verb meaning, to bring or cause strong wind, and the association comes from the waving action created by the shacapa during the venteada.

Vomitivo Ceremony

A purifying ceremony prior to drinking ayahuasca typically using Lemongrass tea or tobacco juice to induce vomiting. See Chapter 10.

Yagé (or Yajé, Yahé)

(pronounced "yah-hey") A Colombian ayahuasca, which is typically strong, thicker.

Ayahuasca Journal

Ayahuasca Journal

Ayahuasca Journal

Ayahuasca Journal

Ayahuasca Journal

Ayahuasca Journal

Citations / References

Chapter 1

1. Pachamama is Quechua and the more natural expression of the medicine. "Pacha" translates to the earth and "mama" translates to mother.
2. Wesley Thoricatha, "What is the Meaning of Psychedelic? Different Terms for Entheogens and What They Mean," *Psychedelic Times*, December 16, 2015, https://psychedelictimes.com/what-is-the-meaning-of-psychedelic-the-difference-between-psychedelics-hallucinogens-and-entheogens/.
3. Ede Frecska, Petra Bokor, and Michael Winkelman, "The Therapeutic Potentials of Ayahuasca: Possible Effects against Various Diseases of Civilization," *Frontiers in Pharmacology 7*, no. 35 (March 2016), https://www.ncbi.nlm.nih.gov/pmc/articles/PMC4773875/.
4. Federico Zamberlan, Camila Sanz, Rocio Martinez Vivot, Carla Pallavicini, Fire Erowid, Earth Erowid, and Enzo Tagliazucchi, "The Varieties of the Psychedelic Experience: A Preliminary Study of the Association Between the Reported Subjective Effects and the Binding Affinity Profiles of Substituted Phenethylamines and Tryptamines," *Frontiers in Integrative Neuroscience* (November 2018), https://www.frontiersin.org/articles/10.3389/fnint.2018.00054/full.
5. "Ayahuasca: Basic Info," ICEERS, last modified 2022, https://www.iceers.org/ayahuasca-basic-info/.
6. Frecska, E., Bokor, P., & Winkelman, M. (2016, March 2). The therapeutic potentials of ayahuasca: Possible effects against various diseases of civilization. Frontiers in pharmacology. from https://www.ncbi.nlm.nih.gov/pmc/articles/PMC4773875
7. Ibid.
8. "Ayahuasca - a mysterious combination of two plants," News, UNI RAO, last modified 2022, https://uniraolodge.com/en/news/ayahuasca-a-mysterious-combination-of-two-plants/.
9. "Ayahuasca and Amazonian Shamanism," Temple of the Way of the Light, last modified 2022,

https://templeofthewayoflight.org/shamanism-ayahuasca/ayahuasca-and-amazonian-shamanism/.
10. Ibid.
11. "What is Shamanism," Dance of the Deer Foundation, last modified 2002, https://www.shamanism.com/what-is-shamanism.
12. Frecska et al., "The Therapeutic Potentials of Ayahuasca,".
13. "Ayahuasca Addiction and Abuse," Ayahuasca Addiction and Dependence, Addiction Center, last modified 2022, https://www.addictioncenter.com/drugs/hallucinogens/ayahuasca/.
14. Robert S. Gable, "Risk assessment of ritual use of oral dimethyltryptamine (DMT) and harmala alkaloids," *Addiction 102,* no. 1 (January 2007), https://pubmed.ncbi.nlm.nih.gov/17207120/.

Chapter 2

1. David Londoño, Jerónimo Mazarrasa, and Marc B. Aixalà, *Towards Better Ayahuasca Practices: A Guide for Organizers and Participants* (ICEERS Foundation, 2019), 17.
2. "Medical Contraindications with Ayahuasca," Temple of the Way of the Light, 2014, https://templeofthewayoflight.org/downloads/Medical-Contraindications-with-Ayahuasca.pdf.
3. "Ayahuasca: Basic Info," ICEERS, last modified 2022, https://www.iceers.org/ayahuasca-basic-info/.
4. Mason Schreck, "Stanislav and Christina Grof: Cartographers of the Psyche," *Maps Bulletin xxi,* no. 1 (May 2011).
5. "Scientists match personality traits with psychedelic experiences," Avalon Magic Plants, published March 2020, https://www.avalonmagicplants.com/sp/blog/scientists-match-personality-traits-with-psychedelic-experiences.
6. "Sit Around The Fire," East Forest, Aquilo Records, last modified September 2, 2021, https://music.eastforest.org/track/sit-around-the-fire-jon-hopkins-ram-dass-east-forest.

Chapter 3

1. Levy, A. (2016, September 5). *The drug of choice for the age of kale.* The New Yorker. https://www.newyorker.com/magazine/2016/09/12/the-ayahuasca-boom-in-the-u-s

Chapter 4

1. "Medical Contraindications with Ayahuasca," Temple of the Way of the Light, 2014, https://templeofthewayoflight.org/downloads/Medical-Contraindications-with-Ayahuasca.pdf.
2. "Serotonin Syndrome," Mayo Clinic, last modified January 22, 2022, https://www.mayoclinic.org/diseases-conditions/serotonin-syndrome/symptoms-causes/syc-20354758#:~:text=Serotonin%20is%20a%20chemical%20that,cause%20death%20if%20not%20treated.
3. "MAOIs and diet: Is it necessary to restrict tyramine?," Mayo Clinic, last modified December 18, 2018, https://www.mayoclinic.org/diseases-conditions/depression/expert-answers/maois/faq-20058035#:~:text=Tyramine%20
4. Alfred Savinelli and John H. Halpern, "MAOI Contraindications," *Multidisciplinary Association for Psychedelic Studies 6*, no. 1, https://maps.org/news-letters/v06n1/06158mao.html.
5. Psychedelic Times Staff, "The Ayahuasca Pre-Diet: How to Prepare for an Ayahuasca Ceremony, According to Shamans," *Psychedelic Times,* August 29, 2019, https://psychedelictimes.com/the-ayahuasca-pre-diet-how-to-prepare-for-an-ayahuasca-ceremony-according-to-shamans/.
6. "Ayahuasca Diet," New Life Ayahuasca, last modified 2022, https://www.newlifeayahuasca.com/ayahuasca-diet.
7. "Dieta Guide," Soul Quest Ayahuasca Church of Mother Earth, 2016, https://www.ayahuascachurches.org/dieta-guide/.
8. "Cannabis," Alcohol, Drugs and Addictive Behaviours Unit, World Health Organization, last modified 2022, https://www.who.int/teams/mental-health-and-substance-use/alcohol-drugs-and-addictive-behaviours/drugs-psychoactive/cannabis.
9. "WHO report says eating processed meat is carcinogenic: Understanding the findings," The Nutrition Source, Harvard T.H. Chan: School of Public Health, November 3, 2015, https://www.hsph.harvard.edu/nutritionsource/2015/11/03/report-says-eating-processed-meat-is-carcinogenic-understanding-the-findings/.
10. Streit, L. (2018, November 7). Mercury in tuna: Is this fish safe to eat? Healthline, from

https://www.healthline.com/nutrition/mercury-in-tuna#bottom-line
11. Center for Food Safety and Applied Nutrition. (n.d.). Mercury levels in commercial fish and shellfish (1990-2012). U.S. Food and Drug Administration from https://www.fda.gov/food/environmental-contaminants-food/mercury-levels-commercial-fish-and-shellfish-1990-2012
12. "Lactose intolerance," Medline Plus, National Library of Medicine, last modified 2010, https://medlineplus.gov/genetics/condition/lactose-intolerance/#:~:text=Approximately%2065%20percent%20of%20the,people%20affected%20in%20these%20communities.
13. Claire Maldarelli, "How much chocolate would you have to eat for it to kill you?" *Popular Science,* February 12, 2021, https://www.popsci.com/chocolate-theobromine-toxic-amount/

Chapter 5

1. Sunny Fitzgerald, "The secret to mindful travel? A walk in the woods," *National Geographic,* October 18, 2019, https://www.nationalgeographic.com/travel/article/forest-bathing-nature-walk-health.
2. Nina Pullano, "Which houseplants purify air? A 1989 NASA study has the answers," *Inverse,* February 15, 2020, https://www.inverse.com/science/which-houseplants-purify-air-nasa-study-answers.

Chapter 7

1. Xavier Francuski, "What Are Ayahuasca Icaros & How Do They Work, *EntheoNation*, 2020, https://entheonation.com/blog/ayahuasca-icaros/.
2. "Ikaros - Songs of the Plants," Temple of the Way of Light, last modified 2022, https://templeofthewayoflight.org/shamanism-ayahuasca/ikaros-songs-of-the-plants/.
3. "Gemstones A-Z," Von Mohs, last modified 2018, https://vonmohs.dk/gemstones/.

Chapter 8

1. "Ego death," Wikipedia, last modified December, 2022, https://en.wikipedia.org/wiki/Ego_death.
2. Psychedelic Times Staff, "The Universal Archetypes of Ayahuasca Dreams and Making Sense of Your Own Visions," *Psychedelics Times*, March 14, 2017, https://psychedelictimes.com/the-universal-archetypes-of-ayahuasca-dreams-and-making-sense-of-your-own-visions/.

Chapter 10

1. "Nicotiana rustica," Wikipedia, last modified December, 2022, https://en.wikipedia.org/wiki/Nicotiana_rustica#:~:text=More%20specifically%2C%20N.,to%20cultures%20around%20the%20world.
2. Psychedelic Times Staff, "From Rapé to Mapacho: Uncovering the Ceremonial and Medicinal Benefits of Sacred Tobacco," *Psychedelic Times*, November 28, 2016, https://psychedelictimes.com/from-rape-to-mapacho-uncovering-ceremonial-medicinal-benefits-sacred-tobacco/.
3. Ibid.
4. Ibid.
5. Guzman, C. (2019, December 9). Introduction to sacred use of Rapé (hapé). YouTube, from https://www.youtube.com/watch?v=UV7q5yqP8d0
6. "Spiritual Growth Using Rapé," Soul Quest, accessed December, 2022, https://www.ayahuascachurches.org/spiritual-growth-using-rape/.
7. Stephen B Stanfill, Andre Luiz Oliveira da Silva, Joseph G Lisko, Tameka S Lawler, Peter Kuklenyik, Robert E Tyx, Elizabeth H Peuchen, Patricia Richter, and Clifford H Watson, "Comprehensive chemical characterization of Rapé tobacco products: Nicotine, un-ionized nicotine, tobacco-specific N'-nitrosamines, polycyclic aromatic hydrocarbons, and flavor constituents," *Food Chem Toxicol 82*, no. 50, https://pubmed.ncbi.nlm.nih.gov/25934468/.
8. "Mambe Medicine," Alma Healing Center, accessed December, 2022, https://almahealingcenter.com/plant-medicine/mambe-coca/.
9. Sharon Kleiman, "Food of the Gods: The Indigenous roots of

chocolate," *Stranger's Guide*, accessed December 2022, https://strangersguide.com/articles/cacao-food-of-the-gods/.
10. Maria Cohut, "Our ancestors were enjoying cocoa over 5,000 years ago," *Medical News Today*, December 22, 2018, https://www.medicalnewstoday.com/articles/323570#:~:text=According%20to%20recent%20evidence%2C%20our,than%20we%20had%20previously%20thought.
11. Jennifer Murray, "The Difference Between Cacao and Cocoa," *The Spruce Eats*, September 13, 2022, https://www.thespruceeats.com/difference-between-cocoa-and-cacao-3376438#:~:text=Eats%20%2F%20Julia%20Hartbeck-,Cacao%20vs.,minimally%20processed%20with%20no%20additives.
12. Jillian Levy, "Top 5 Theobromine Benefits (Plus Side Effects, Supplements & More)", *Dr. Axe*, February 6, 2020, https://draxe.com/nutrition/theobromine-benefits/.
13. Sananga Canada, "Complete Guide to Sananga Eye Drops - Traditional Usage, Effects and Benefits," *Sananga Canada*, August 22, 2020, https://sananga.ca/sananga/complete-guide-to-sananga-eye-drops/.
14. Ibid.
15. Rachel Nall, "What are the health benefits of lemongrass tea?," *Medical News Today*, October 24, 2018, https://www.medicalnewstoday.com/articles/321969.

Chapter 11

1. Ede Frecska, Petra Bokor, and Michael Winkelman, "The Therapeutic Potentials of Ayahuasca: Possible Effects against Various Diseases of Civilizations," *Frontiers in Pharmacology 7*, no. 35, March 2, 2016, https://www.ncbi.nlm.nih.gov/pmc/articles/PMC4773875/#B70.
2. In this context, "scientific" refers to the dominant epistemology of Western culture. Many in our time are rightly critical of the limitations of Western science, such as its assumptions of objectivism, materialism, and dualism. A more empowering and sensible approach to science may be to perceive yourself as a scientist in your journey of healing: What does the data of your direct experience tell you? What experiments are you doing in your own life?

3. Fernanda Palhano-Fontes, Katia C Andrade, Luis F Tofoli, Antonio C Santos, Jose Alexandre S Crippa, Jaime E C Hallak, Sidarta Ribeiro and Draulio B de Araujo, "The psychedelic state induced by ayahuasca modulates the activity and connectivity of the default mode network," *PLoS One 10,* no. 2, February 18, 2015, https://pubmed.ncbi.nlm.nih.gov/25693169/#:~:text=Self%2Dorien ted%20mental%20activity%20has,Ayahuasca%20in%20ten%20ex perienced%20subjects.
4. Daniel Perkins, Broc A. Pagni, Jerome Sarris, Paulo C. R. Barbosa and Richard Chenhall, "Changes in mental health, wellbeing and personality following ayahuasca consumption: Results of a naturalistic longitudinal study," *Front Pharmacol. 13,* Oct 26, 2022, https://www.ncbi.nlm.nih.gov/pmc/articles/PMC9643165/.
5. Psychology and Religion: West and East (The Collected Works of C. G. Jung, Volume 11)
6. Todd Thatcher, "Can Emotional Trauma Cause Brain Damage?", *Highland Springs,* February 4, 2019, https://highlandspringsclinic.org/can-emotional-trauma-cause-brain-damage/#:~:text=When%20affected%20by%20PTSD%2C%20the, event%20a%20person%20suffered%20from.
7. Itzhak Beery, "Soul Healing: Unifying the Lost Part of Yourself with Your Whole Being," *Kripalu,* 2017, https://kripalu.org/resources/soul-healing-unifying-lost-part-yourself-your-whole-being#:~:text=Across%20shamanic%20traditions%2C%20soul%2 0loss,%2C%20emotional%2C%20and%20mental%20well%2D.
8. Harald Brussow, "What is health?," *Microb Biotechnol 6,* no. 4, July 2013, https://www.ncbi.nlm.nih.gov/pmc/articles/PMC3917469/.
9. Lloyd I. Sederer, "What does "Rat Park" Teach Us About Addiction?," *Psychiatric Times,* June 9, 2019, https://www.psychiatrictimes.com/view/what-does-rat-park-teach-us-about-addiction.
10. Michael Pollan, *This is Your Mind on Plants* (Penguin Publishing Group, 2021), 235-236. Kindle Edition.

Made in the USA
Monee, IL
19 October 2024